SOBRIETY

IS A TEAM SPORT

SOBRIETY
IS A TEAM SPORT

STILLTOM

Library of Congress Control Number: 2024925223

ISBN: 979-8-89228-340-3   (Paperback)
ISBN: 979-8-89228-341-0   (Hardcover)
ISBN: 979-8-89228-339-7   (eBook)

Book Ordering Information:
Atticus Publishing
548 Market St PMB 70756
San Francisco, CA 94104
(888) 208-9296
info@atticuspublishing.com
www.atticuspublishing.com

Printed in the United States of America

CONTENTS

DEDICATION

THIS BOOK IS DEDICATED TO MY WIFE OF 56 YEARS, WENDY. We met as teenagers and fell in love quickly. We married while still in college, and through her determination, we managed to stay together even as my alcoholism deepened and my participation as a husband and father to our two daughters deteriorated. Her eventual ultimatum, following a drunk driving charge, was the wake-up call that led to my recovery. Today, we are more in love than ever and continue to work on leaving the past in the past. Recovery is something worth celebrating.

I also want to extend my deepest gratitude to Tim Sherman, whose incredible talent breathed life into this manuscript through his stunning sketches. Tim, your artistry has done more than enhance these pages—it has brought them to life in ways words alone could never achieve. Every stroke, every detail reflects the heart and soul of this journey. Your creative vision has added a depth and beauty that speaks directly to the emotions of this story.

ACKNOWLEDGEMENT

FRANK PARKHURST WAS A KEY FIGURE IN THE EARLY DAYS of Alcoholics Anonymous, especially during the 1930s and 1940s. Though specific details about his early life are scarce, his influence is undeniable. Parkhurst entered AA at a time when alcoholism was heavily stigmatized and misunderstood, and his personal experiences with addiction fueled his passion to help others facing similar struggles. Active from the organization's formative years, he stood firmly for AA's core values of mutual aid and community support, championing its non-profit foundation. Parkhurst believed that any attempt to profit from AA would undermine its integrity, insisting that the focus remain solely on helping individuals find freedom from alcoholism.

In public speaking and writing, Parkhurst also worked to destigmatize addiction, presenting alcoholism as a disease and promoting recovery as an achievable goal. His advocacy for non-commercial, service-oriented recovery left a profound mark on AA's guiding principles—principles that continue to inspire countless people today. Altruism, community, and the power of shared experiences, all values Parkhurst championed, remain central to AA's mission and to the millions who find solace in its fellowship.

In traditional AA meetings the proper introduction at the beginning of any meeting would be, "Hello, my name is Tom, and I'm an alcoholic." This practice is 90 years old, and I think outdated. So for years I've simply said "Hello I'm Still Tom."—that was the relevance of my choosing this Pen Name. This choice reflects my disappointment with a practice dating back nearly 90 years: the expectation to name a specific addiction and avoid using one's last name, as if to shield ourselves from embarrassment. I understand that, in its time, this tradition may have protected jobs and reputations within communities and churches. But today, I believe that our ability to embrace our identities fully and without shame is essential to finding peace in recovery. After all, Sobriety Is a Team Sport.

DESIRE... CRAVING... ADDICTION... RECOVERY

INTRODUCTION

*S*OBRIETY *IS A TEAM SPORT* OFFERS A SCOUTING REPORT, A GAME plan, and a scorecard for the journey to recovery from addiction. My intention is not just to help those of us struggling with addiction but also to support the families, friends, and loved ones who stand by our side. Team participation in sobriety means recognizing and using all the resources available to us. It's about working together, lifting each other up, and building a community that supports a healthier, more serene life. This approach goes beyond just recovery from alcoholism, it applies to all aspects of life. Whether in work, family, or friendships, collective efforts strengthen both individual and group well-being.

When it comes to alcoholism, this book emphasizes the importance of both community and individual support systems. Participating in recovery groups, like *Alcoholics Anonymous*, can provide a network of people who understand the struggle and are walking a similar path. These groups often become more than just a support system; they take on the role of a higher power for many, offering the comfort and strength of a close-knit family. Within these teams, there's a sense of belonging—a shared knowledge that no one has to face this battle alone.

Kris Kristofferson, reflecting on his own battle with addiction, once said: *'I never thought I'd live past 30. I could have ended up dead at any time, for a couple of years. It was Jack Daniels, then it was tequila, then it was anything when I was performing. I couldn't imagine getting up and doing it without drinking. I remember feeling that it could very easily be my wife and kids crying over me. I quit drinking because I didn't want to die before my daughter grew up.'*

His words remind us that the stakes in recovery are often about more than just ourselves. It's about the people we love, the lives we touch, and the future we want to build. A supportive network of family and friends plays a crucial role in this process, offering not just encouragement but also accountability. They become a mirror, reflecting our progress and our setbacks, helping us to stay focused on the path ahead.

Sobriety is not something we achieve in isolation—it's a team sport. And in this game, the goal is not just personal victory but collective healing. We lean on each other, and in doing so, we find the strength to continue, even when the road gets tough. This book is designed to help you not only recruit your winning team but also learn how to manage and lead that team. Together, through community and connection, we can create a roadmap to sobriety, one that guides us through not just addiction, but every challenge life throws our way.

Team involvement is a cornerstone of recovery. It not only keeps motivation alive but also provides the emotional support that so many of us need. When you're part of a team, you're not just playing for yourself—you're playing for everyone around you, and they're playing for you. In sobriety, this is critical. Professional guidance can help individuals develop coping strategies, address underlying issues related to addiction, and, most importantly, teach them how to play a new game. For many of us, alcoholism taught us how to be solo players. But recovery is a team sport, and with the right coaching, we can learn how to play alongside others, supporting each other through the ups and downs.

Participating in team activities, whether it's exercise, group therapy, or shared hobbies, doesn't just replace negative habits with positive ones. It fosters something deeper—a sense of community and belonging. In these environments, honest conversations are encouraged. Sharing struggles builds trust, and having that trust reduces the feelings of isolation that so often accompany addiction. It's a powerful shift to go from feeling alone to realizing you have a team behind you, ready to support you at every turn.

Recovery, at its heart, is about connection. By viewing sobriety as a team effort, individuals can draw strength from the people around them, knowing that every victory, big or small, is celebrated as a collective win. The team celebrates when someone makes it through a tough day without drinking. They're there to listen when cravings become overwhelming. They provide accountability when life throws curveballs. It's not about facing struggles alone—it's about relying on the strength of the team, and in turn, becoming stronger yourself.

This book will not only help you recruit your winning team but also guide you on how to manage and strengthen it. Together, we will create a strategy that enhances your journey toward serenity, sobriety, and, ultimately, a life filled with purpose and connection. This team-based approach applies not just to recovery but to all areas of life—work, family, friendships—because, when we work together, we thrive together.

CHAPTER ONE

The Coach:
Learn New Reactions

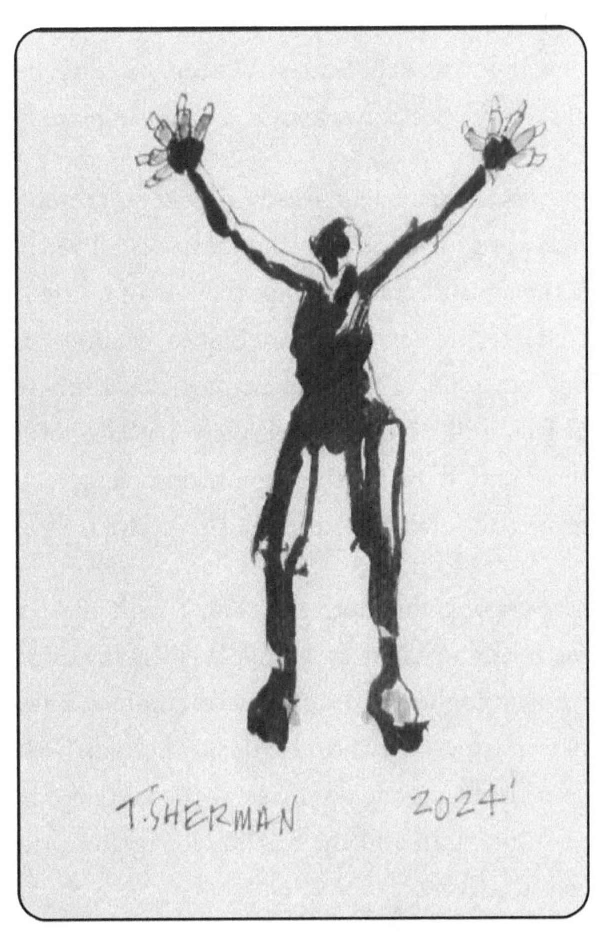

NOTHING IS EVER ENOUGH... AND WE WANT IT TO NEVER stop. To someone who has never battled addiction, this phrase might sound confusing, maybe even nonsensical. But for those of us who have lived with alcoholism, this statement hits home in a way that's difficult to describe. It's not just words—it's a reflection of a powerful, insatiable craving that lives deep inside us.

This phrase points to a fundamental part of human nature, one that's often magnified in those of us struggling with addiction: the constant hunger for more. More alcohol, more escape, more of that fleeting sense of satisfaction that never truly lasts. It's a hunger that never seems to be satisfied, no matter how much we consume, how much we achieve, or how much we experience. We keep reaching, keep chasing, yet the fulfillment we seek always slips just out of reach.

The second part of the statement—*we* want it never to stop—is perhaps even more revealing. It speaks to our deep-seated fear of endings. Whether it's the end of a relationship, the loss of a loved one, or the closing of a chapter in our lives, we cling to what we have because we fear what comes next. We fear change, the unknown, and the possibility of facing life without the crutch that alcohol has become. We want to hold onto those fleeting moments of pleasure, even though we know they're temporary, because the alternative feels unbearable.

This relentless craving for more, combined with the fear of losing what we have, forms a vicious cycle that keeps many of us trapped in addiction. And while these feelings may be common among those of us with addiction issues, they are also deeply human. We all, in some way, struggle with the paradox of desire—the longing for something we can never fully attain and the fear of letting go of the things we think we need to survive.

Throughout this book, I will share many of the thoughts and experiences that are common to those of us living with addiction. My goal is not just to explain the patterns we find ourselves in, but to help you understand that you're not alone in feeling this way. Whether you're struggling with alcoholism or another form of addiction, these cravings and fears are shared by many. Together, we will explore the paths to recovery, understanding that while the journey may be challenging, it is possible to break free from the cycle and find peace.

The "pleasure treadmill" refers to the constant need we have to quickly return to a stable level of happiness, no matter the highs or lows we experience. For those of us who have struggled with addiction, this treadmill is all too familiar. Many of us spent years running on it, thinking we could outrun the dissatisfaction that seemed to chase us. But no matter how much we drank, how many moments of escape we found, we never quite reached the fulfillment we were seeking. It always felt like something was missing.

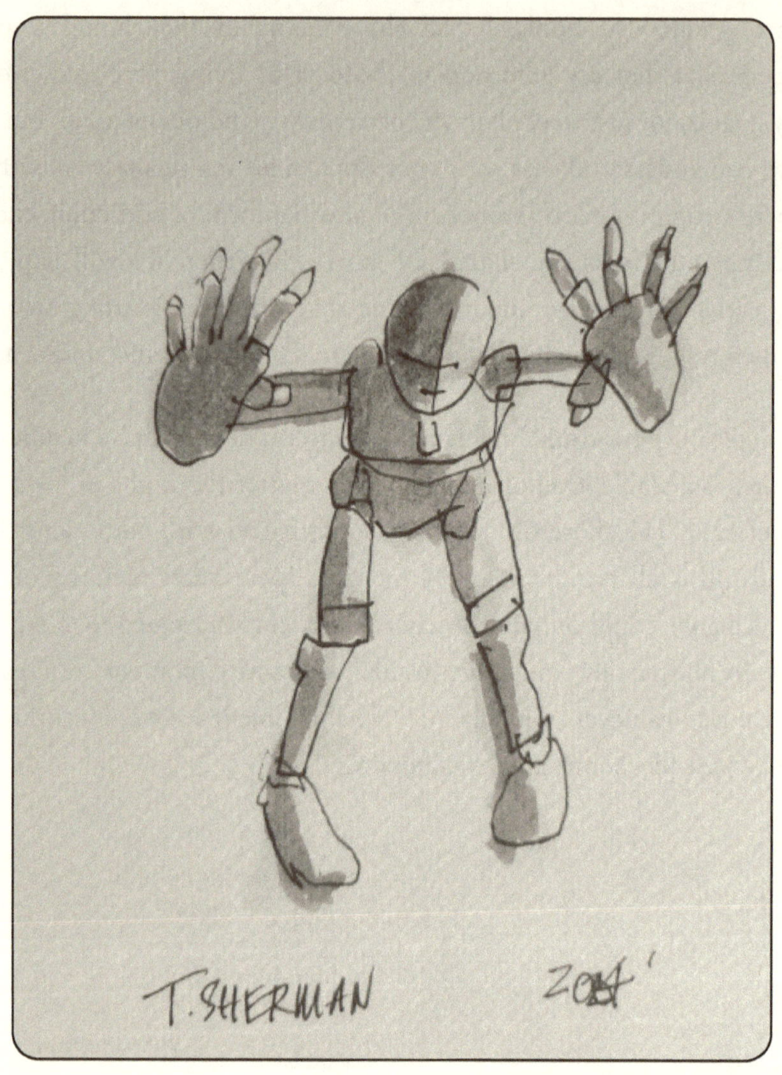

This endless pursuit—the feeling that nothing is ever enough—captures the paradox of human desire. We seek, we acquire, and yet, we often find ourselves unsatisfied. We keep looking for more, believing that the next drink, the next experience, or the next accomplishment will finally fill that void inside us. And still, there's a reluctance to let go of that chase. We're afraid of what might happen if we stop running, stop seeking, and just be.

This struggle between desire and contentment is something many of us face, whether we're battling addiction or just trying to find peace in our everyday lives. It's a balancing act, one that highlights the importance of mindfulness, gratitude, and self-awareness. These are the tools that can help us step off the treadmill, pause, and finally find the satisfaction we've been chasing.

In the pages that follow, I'll explore the causes behind this relentless craving—the deeper roots of addiction that go beyond the physical and dive into the emotional and psychological. But for now, understand this: the treadmill doesn't define us. We can step off, regain our footing, and begin the process of healing.

Throughout our lives, we encounter all kinds of lists. They help us organize, remember, and track what's important. Whether it's a grocery list, a daily schedule, or a sequence of steps to complete a task, lists bring order to chaos. Much like the literature of Alcoholics Anonymous, this book will also contain many lists—some of them researched through Artificial Intelligence, others inspired by my personal journey.

It's remarkable to think that nearly 100 years ago, when Alcoholics Anonymous was first formed, no one could have imagined that technology like AI might one day play a role in recovery. But here we are. As we embrace the future, these lists, along with my personal story, are meant to serve as resources for you—a map guiding you toward your own discovery of sobriety, through mindful and sober living.

The lists, like the ones you'll find in this book, aren't just about steps to follow. They are reminders of the structure and support available to you. They serve as touchpoints, helping you stay grounded and focused on the path ahead. My hope is that these lists, combined with the lessons I've learned along the way, will provide you with the tools to build your own team, create your own strategies, and ultimately, find peace in your recovery.

The first list I want to share is ancient—so ancient, in fact, that it predates Christ by hundreds of years, long before the New Testament or many of the major religions we know today. It is one of the oldest known pieces of writing, originally recorded in the ancient Pali language. Later in this book, we will explore how this ancient list holds relevance for us in recovery, offering spiritual and practical insights. This list goes by several names: The Five Remembrances, The Five Contemplations, or The Five Reflections, depending on the language used to interpret it.

The Five Remembrances serve as a stark reminder of the truths we all must face in life. Here they are:

1. I am of nature to grow old. There is no way to escape growing old.

2. I am of nature to have ill health; there is no way to escape having ill health.

3. I am of nature to die. There is no way to escape death.

4. All that is dear to me and everyone I love are of nature to change. There is no way to escape being separated from them.

5. My deeds are my closest companions. I am the beneficiary of my deeds. My deeds are the ground on which I stand.

At first glance, these reflections might seem harsh. They offer no soothing comfort, no promise of eternal life, no assurance of heavenly rewards. In ancient times, exposure to this list didn't necessarily lead people toward immediate solace or spiritual peace. Instead, it inspired something else—a need to seek out a deeper understanding of life, to create paths toward salvation and spiritual meaning.

For those of us in recovery, these reflections can hit close to home. Addiction often arises out of our fear of facing these universal truths. We fear growing old, we dread ill health, and we run from the idea of death. We cling to the people and things we love, afraid of losing them, and we often act in ways we regret, unsure of how to face the consequences. The truth is, alcohol may have helped us numb those fears temporarily, but it never freed us from them.

These ancient reflections force us to confront the things we cannot change about life—and in recovery, that's something we learn to do. The Five Remembrances remind us that while we cannot escape these realities, we can take control of our deeds. Our actions are the foundation of our lives, and in sobriety, we have the power to shape them. By living mindfully, accepting change, and taking responsibility for what we do, we build a new foundation—one that can sustain us through the challenges ahead.

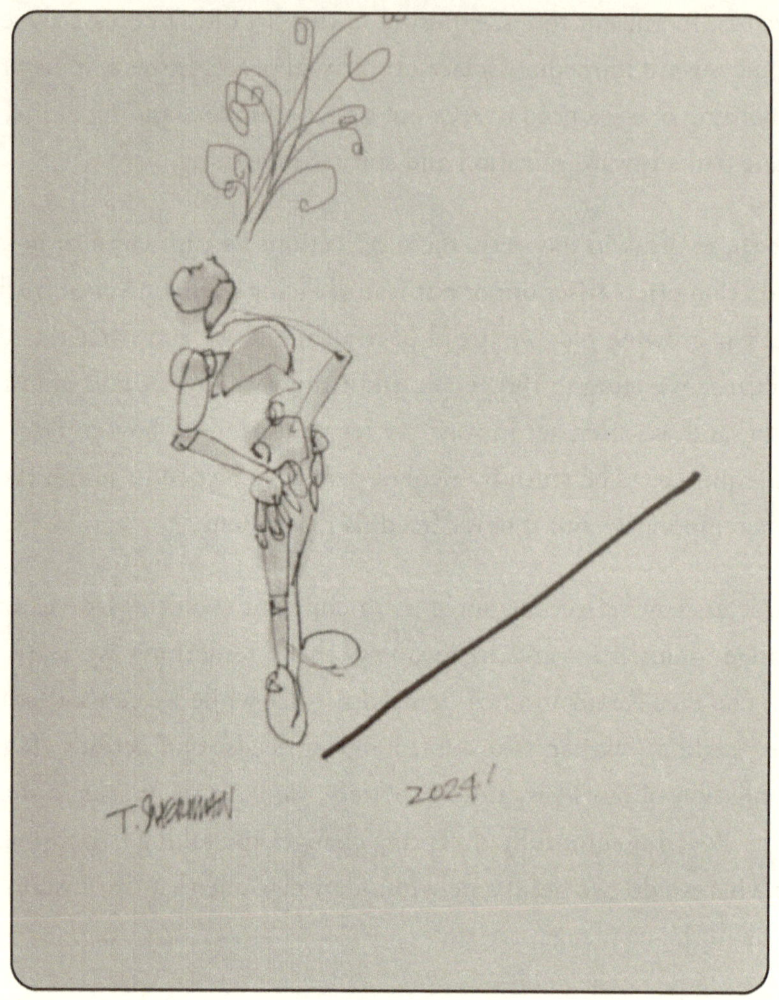

Recovery doesn't promise an escape from the realities of life, but it offers a new way to face them. These reflections, though ancient, remain as relevant today as they were centuries ago. They encourage us to embrace the truths of life rather than run from them, and in doing so, they help us find peace in the present moment.

Early in sobriety, the veterans—the ones who've walked this road a little longer—have a responsibility to step up and offer guidance to the rookies. This journey is complex, and the stakes are high.

Understanding the rules of the game, the strategies that help an alcoholic stay sober, can mean the difference between relapsing and surviving. I recently attended a speaker meeting where the speaker, just one year sober, shared her story. She had met and married her spouse during her first year of sobriety, and while she radiated happiness, she began recounting her many struggles—car accidents, deaths in the family, financial hardships, and multiple divorces that had led to her relapses over the years. Her vulnerability was palpable, and as much as I wanted to root for her, I couldn't help but feel worried. Newfound sobriety is fragile, almost naive in its optimism.

And that fragility isn't to be dismissed. For anyone in the early stages of recovery, stress, social situations, or even the familiar environments where we once drank can trigger a relapse. Emotional challenges like anxiety, depression, or unresolved trauma often rear their heads, making the pull of alcohol feel insurmountable. The influence of friends or family who still drink can further weaken resolve. And when support from recovery groups or loved ones feels insufficient, we may find ourselves standing on shaky ground, vulnerable to intense cravings that threaten to break our commitment to sobriety.

Another challenge is the false sense of security that can arise after a few months of sobriety. We feel strong, confident, and invincible, as if the worst is behind us. But that can lead to risky behaviors and complacency, leaving us open to relapse. Sobriety is not a destination—it's a daily practice, one that requires us to navigate the challenges life throws our way with care and humility.

In those moments, when the path feels uncertain, we must return to the fundamentals of recovery. Our personal serenity is built upon how well we navigate the emotional, spiritual, and physical challenges that come our way. It's a map of our own making, informed by the spiritual or religious guidance we choose to follow and the behaviors we commit to. And for many, this map leads to healing—a path that, while difficult, offers the promise of recovery if we stay the course and learn to lean on our team.

Recovery isn't just about abstaining from alcohol. It's about creating a life that supports your sobriety, finding meaning in the journey, and surrounding yourself with people who hold you accountable. It's about knowing when to ask for help, understanding that you don't have to do this alone, and finding comfort in the idea that together, as a team, we can make it through the darkest of times.

You can't truly understand me if you can't first understand yourself. Recovery, much like life, is deeply personal. And while no two paths are the same, there are common threads that tie us together—shared struggles, shared victories. This book, Sobriety Is *a* Team Sport, is filled with players ready to support you in finding your own personal serenity, and ultimately, sobriety. The team you build around you, the "players" you choose, and the starting lineup you put on the field are critical for your success. Sobriety isn't a solo game—it's about teamwork, strategy, and support.

The Serenity Prayer, written by Reinhold Niebuhr in 1932, has long been a cornerstone for many of us in recovery. But its message reaches far beyond just those of us who are alcoholics. It reads:

"God, Grant me the serenity to accept the things I cannot change, courage to change the things I can, and wisdom to know the difference."

This simple, powerful prayer isn't just for the recovery community—it's a guide for life. It's a call to mindfulness, to live fully in the present moment, accepting what is, and finding the strength to change what can be changed. The Serenity Prayer is, in many ways, an introduction to mindfulness itself, an ancient practice that has become the foundation for much of modern psychology and wellness, not just for sobriety.

Mindfulness is about being present. It's about noticing your breath, your thoughts, your feelings—without judgment, without needing to change them. Its roots can be traced back to ancient Buddhist teachings, particularly the importance of breathwork. Breath connects us to the present moment. It grounds us, calms us, and reminds us that we are here, now.

I learned this firsthand from my teacher, Thich Nhat Hanh, who passed away last year. Thich Nhat Hanh taught me about breath awareness and its immense power—not just as a tool for relaxation, but as a pathway to understanding the deeper currents of life. I am deeply thankful for those lessons. And I have found that, in recovery, "taking a deep breath" is not just good advice for children throwing tantrums or for managing moments of panic—it's an essential tool for staying grounded in the present moment.

In recovery, as in life, we need to constantly return to the present. The past is done, and the future is not yet written. We only have now. And while this may seem like a simple truth, it's one that can make all the difference when the road gets rough. Mindfulness reminds us to breathe, to stay present, and to respond to life as it is happening. This practice of being present is essential for navigating sobriety, because it helps us manage the anxiety of what may come and the regrets of what has already been.

Building your team—choosing the right players to help you on your journey—is about finding those people and practices that help keep you grounded in the present moment. Mindfulness, breathwork, the Serenity Prayer—these are your teammates, just as much as your recovery group, your friends, or your family. Together, they create a roster of support that helps you navigate the difficult moments and celebrate the victories.

Sobriety is a team sport, and the more players you have who help you stay mindful, focused, and present, the stronger your team becomes. Take a deep breath. Trust in the moment. And know that with the right team behind you, you can face whatever challenges come your way.

One of the simplest ways to ground yourself, to stay connected to the present moment, is by following your breath. It's an act we often take for granted, something we do automatically. But by paying attention to your breath, you can create a space of calm within yourself, no matter what chaos is swirling around you.

Here's how you can practice it:

Find a comfortable place where you can relax without being disturbed. This might be a cozy chair in your living room, a quiet corner at the end of a busy day, or even a peaceful spot outdoors. If it feels right, close your eyes. Take a few deep breaths to help settle your mind, letting the rhythm of your breathing bring you into the present.

Now, begin to focus your attention on your breath. Notice the cool air entering your nostrils and the warm air as you exhale. Feel the rise and fall of your chest, or the gentle expansion and contraction of your abdomen as you breathe. Pick a detail that resonates with you—whether it's the sound of your breath, the sensation of air passing through your body, or the movement of your chest—and simply stay with it.

It's normal for your mind to wander, especially if you're just beginning this practice. Thoughts will pop up—about what you need to do tomorrow, or replaying moments from earlier today. When that happens, gently bring your attention back to your breath. Don't judge yourself for losing focus. Just guide yourself back, like a caring coach reminding you to stay in the game.

Continue following your breath for a few minutes, or for as long as feels comfortable. Fully experience each inhale and exhale, without rushing or forcing anything. Let it all unfold naturally.

When you're ready to finish, take a few deeper breaths and slowly open your eyes, easing yourself back into the world. Notice how you feel after spending this time focusing on your breath. Does your body feel a little lighter? Is your mind a bit quieter? Like a drink finally settling after you've stirred it, you may notice a newfound clarity.

This simple exercise can be done throughout your day, whenever you need it. And like a great teammate, your breath is always with you, offering support whenever you need to slow down, refocus, or find calm in the midst of life's challenges.

Breathing is something most of us take for granted—until, suddenly, we can't. My father was a heavy smoker who developed severe emphysema. I watched as the simple act of drawing breath became a battle for him, a daily struggle that consumed his final years. My niece, too, had severe asthma as a child. For her and her parents, breathing was always on their minds, a constant presence in their lives that couldn't be ignored. Then there was my good friend, who passed away while waiting for a lung transplant. His months of suffering, as each breath became a painful reminder of what he was losing, were agonizing to witness.

I, too, had my own brush with respiratory illness when I contracted severe RSV from my grandson. It landed me in a situation I never expected—working as a patient ambassador for a drug company. Until that experience, I had no idea how critical just a few percentage points in blood oxygen levels could be. Breath awareness, I learned, is more than just a tool for mindfulness; it's a vital health practice, something we should all pay attention to before it's too late.

Our lives are quite literally bookended by breath. The very first thing we do when we enter the world is take that first in-breath, and the last thing we'll ever do is release one final exhale. Breath is life itself.

This brings to mind a quote from my old Spartan football coach, Duffy Daughtery: *'Winning and losing isn't a matter of life and death… It's much more important than that.'*

In recovery, we know that our survival hinges on far more than just staying sober. It's about the whole picture—laughing, crying, feeling everything that comes with being alive. And nowhere is this clearer than in the many recovery meetings I've attended over the years.

If you've been in those rooms, you know the truth: what happens before and after the meetings is often as important as the meetings themselves. You can feel it in the conversations in the parking lot, the cups of coffee shared afterward, the hugs exchanged when someone is struggling. The meeting doesn't end when the clock says it does, because we're not just attending for ourselves—we're showing up for each other. We create families there, ones that don't rely on biology, but on shared experiences and mutual support.

These groups become the emotional support systems so many of us lacked growing up. Week after week, we meet in the same rooms, at the same time, with the same faces, and we build something sacred—a place where stuffing our emotions isn't allowed, where laughter and tears are both welcome, and where the journey of sobriety is shared.

Recovery isn't just about stopping the drink; it's about finding a way to live fully in a world that keeps moving, even when it feels overwhelming. And just like breath is essential to life, these support systems—these families we create—are essential to our sobriety.

The bond that forms in recovery groups, the compassion we share with each other, is unlike anything I've ever experienced elsewhere. It's raw, honest, and profoundly human. In those rooms, we come together not just to talk, but to listen, to laugh, to cry. Every moment becomes crucial for our recovery, allowing us to fully live our lives with a renewed sense of purpose.

Many of us who became alcoholics missed important emotional lessons along the way—somewhere between childhood and adulthood, we lost the ability to fully process our emotions. Mindfulness helps us reclaim that. Learning to live in the present not only makes sobriety more manageable but also helps us untangle the knots of our chaotic pasts. The present, free from the weight of attachments, can become a place of peace, where stress is kept at bay.

And while mindfulness and emotional honesty are critical, so is humor. Humor is a necessary teammate. There's a reason locker rooms are filled with banter—it binds people together. Laughter connects us in ways that words alone can't. Years ago, I had the privilege of attending a speech by Desmond Tutu in Kalamazoo, Michigan. You may know him as a South African Anglican bishop and an activist who fought tirelessly against Apartheid. His life was filled with unimaginable hardship—jailed numerous times, constantly in danger—yet he was one of the funniest speakers I've ever heard.

Tutu didn't let the weight of his struggles define him. He spoke out for peace, justice, and equality, all while cracking jokes and lightening the hearts of those around him. At the time, I didn't fully grasp the magnitude of his resilience. Here was a man who had endured the brutal realities of fighting against an oppressive regime, and still, he found joy in the midst of it all.

That's something we need in recovery, too. We're often dealing with the harsh realities of our pasts—failed relationships, job losses, broken families—but that doesn't mean we can't laugh. Recovery meetings reflect that balance. We share our deepest pains, yes, but we also share moments of joy and humor. There's healing in that laughter, just as there is in the tears.

Humor isn't just a way to deflect pain. It's a way to connect, to show that we're still here, still human, and still fighting. The support groups we form during recovery become a kind of chosen family, the emotional support system we lacked while growing up. Week after week, we gather in the same rooms, often with the same faces, and over time, those meetings become a safe haven—a place where we can finally be ourselves, without fear of judgment.

It's in these moments, when we share both our laughter and our pain, that we truly begin to heal. And it's through this bond, this unbreakable sense of compassion, that we discover the strength to keep moving forward.

Joining Nelson Mandela and other political martyrs in their fight for justice, Desmond Tutu exemplified the ability to face adversity without turning away. In Buddhism, this is known as "facing Mara"—the practice of confronting difficulties directly, without the need to anticipate outcomes or retreat into fear. For many of us in recovery, this practice of mindful confrontation can become a powerful tool, enabling us to stand in the face of addiction without being overwhelmed by its pull.

The same strength that helped these leaders survive political and personal turmoil can also be applied to our recovery journey. Facing challenges head-on—whether they stem from addiction, trauma, or fear—allows us to find a way through them. Understanding that all things are impermanent can give us the perspective to compartmentalize our troubles and prevent them from taking over our lives. Recovery isn't about avoiding pain, but learning to move through it with clarity, patience, and self-compassion.

Two other great spiritual leaders who shared this mindset were the Dalai Lama and Thich Nhat Hanh. Despite their different traditions—Tibetan Buddhism for the Dalai Lama and Zen Buddhism for Thich Nhat Hanh—their teachings emphasized similar values: love, compassion, mindfulness, and the pursuit of peace. Their bond was one of mutual respect, rooted in the understanding that suffering is universal but how we respond to it can transform our lives.

I once heard a charming story about these two spiritual giants that illustrates the lighter side of mindfulness. At Thich Nhat Hanh's birthday party, he and the Dalai Lama engaged in a playful exchange—stealing each other's hats, laughing like children. It was a moment that humanized them, reminding us that even those who carry the weight of the world on their shoulders can find joy in the simplest moments. It showed that mindfulness isn't just about stillness and reflection; it's also about being fully present, fully alive, and open to joy, even in the midst of struggle.

This story serves as a beautiful reminder: serious people can laugh. Humor is as essential to our recovery as mindfulness. In fact, humor binds us together as much as shared pain does. Recovery meetings are full of laughter—not just because we find humor in our shared experiences, but because laughing together builds connection. It helps us process the challenges of life with a lighter heart.

Mindfulness, humor, and resilience are critical in our recovery journey. Pain is inevitable, but suffering is optional. The ability to face our struggles, as Tutu, the Dalai Lama, and Thich Nhat Hanh have shown, can help us navigate the hardest parts of life with grace. By learning to let go of attachments, we allow ourselves to live fully in the present moment—a place where peace, clarity, and sobriety can thrive.

One of the most powerful lessons that helps us understand the distinction between pain and suffering comes from an ancient Buddhist story, often shared in mindfulness and recovery groups like ACT (Accountability-Connection-Treatment). It's known as the *Parable of the Second Arrow.*

Imagine you're walking through the woods, and suddenly you're struck by an arrow. The arrow hits you in the arm, and it hurts—a deep, physical pain that immediately demands your attention. This is the first arrow: the unavoidable pain that comes with life. It's real, and it hurts.

But then, something else happens. Your mind takes over and begins to spin. You start thinking, What if I bleed to death? *What if this wound gets infected? What will happen to my family if I don't make it back? Will they be okay without me?* Your thoughts race toward every worst-case scenario imaginable. This is the second arrow: suffering—the story we create around the pain.

Buddha's teaching here is simple: while we can't always avoid the first arrow (the physical or emotional pain), the suffering caused by the second arrow is often self-inflicted. It's our mind's reaction to the pain—our anxieties, fears, and catastrophic thoughts—that magnify the suffering. And it's this second arrow we have the power to control.

In recovery, this distinction between pain and suffering becomes crucial. The pain of addiction—whether it's withdrawal, cravings, or the fallout of our actions—can feel overwhelming. But it's what we do next that determines whether we stay in the suffering or begin to heal.

Recovery teaches us that while we can't always escape the pain, we can change how we respond to it. By practicing mindfulness, we can learn to face our pain without adding layers of suffering. We can feel the hurt but not let it spiral into despair or hopelessness. Mindfulness teaches us to stay present, to breathe through the discomfort, and to trust that the pain will pass.

The story of the second arrow reminds us that in life, pain is inevitable, but suffering is optional. This wisdom is essential for anyone on the journey to sobriety. Learning how to distinguish between the two is one of the most powerful tools we can have in recovery.

Understanding the *Parable* of the *Second Arrow* offers us a powerful insight into how we often add unnecessary suffering to our lives. It's about resistance, denial, and our reaction to the pain we inevitably face. In many recovery programs, including ACT (Accountability-Connection-Treatment), we learn a valuable formula: *Pain × Resistance = Suffering*. As an old algebra teacher, I love formulas—they simplify complex ideas. In this case, the more we resist, deny, or fight against the pain that already exists, the more suffering we create for ourselves.

Let's unpack this with an example. Imagine a difficult situation: you may be feeling sadness, anxiety, or anger—internal experiences that we all face. It could also be a physical challenge like chronic pain. These are the first arrows—the unavoidable difficulties in life. But then, we add the second arrow—our thoughts spiraling into worst case scenarios, our resistance to accepting what's already happening. This is where suffering begins.

So, how do we minimize the suffering? How do we face the pain without adding layers of distress? Here are a few thoughts:

1. **Remember the story.** Whenever you're facing a difficult situation, pause and reflect on the second arrow. Are your thoughts or behaviors adding to your suffering? Recognizing this is the first step toward reducing unnecessary suffering.

2. **Respond with compassion.** When you feel pain, whether emotional or physical, place your hand gently where it hurts. This act of self-kindness can help create space for the pain instead of resisting it. It's a simple yet powerful way to soothe yourself.

3. **Assess your level of acceptance.** Rate how much you are accepting your current reality, perhaps on a scale from one to ten. Then, ask yourself, "How can I gently increase my acceptance of this difficult experience?" The more you accept the present moment, the less suffering you'll endure.

The second arrow story reminds us of the difference between pain and suffering. Pain is inevitable, but suffering is optional. This perspective is invaluable in recovery, teaching us that while we can't always avoid the arrows of life, we can choose how we respond to them. It's an essential part of navigating our journey to sobriety. If this story resonates with you, consider looking up the original sutta—it's a beautiful teaching with endless wisdom.

I recently visited a group sobriety website where I read a post from someone with 12 years of continuous sobriety. Despite his long track record, he admitted to facing challenges that were beginning to stir thoughts of drinking again. He shared about the pressure of a demanding work schedule, the stress of living in a precarious housing situation, and the strain of intense marital problems. These are the real-life battles we face in recovery—constant, unrelenting challenges that can lead us to think that the old escape of alcohol might offer relief. But we know deep down, and so does he, that alcohol would only make things worse.

Alcohol is cunning, baffling, powerful—and, most dangerously, patient. It waits for the moment when we are most vulnerable, whispering that maybe just one drink will help. That's why it's crucial for those of us in recovery to hear these stories, stories that serve as constant reminders of the ever-present risk of falling back into old patterns. Before a relapse, there is always a slow drift back into familiar, harmful behaviors.

Hearing these struggles is more than just a reminder. It's a lifeline. It's a way for all of us to gain strength from each other's experiences, to find hope in knowing that we are not alone in our fight. As we listen to these stories, we remind ourselves that we're not just struggling individually—we are part of a team, and together, we can weather the storms that life throws at us.

We need to remember: relapse doesn't start with the drink—it starts with the thoughts that lead to it. By recognizing the warning signs in others, we can see them in ourselves. These shared experiences keep us vigilant, grounded, and aware of the path we must continue walking together.

CHAPTER TWO

THE SCOUT: STUDY THE OPPONENT TENDENCIES

ADDICTION HAS INFILTRATED NEARLY EVERY CORNER OF OUR lives, affecting not just individuals but entire families and communities. The sheer scale of suffering is staggering, and our collective acceptance of this crisis is essential. Yet, as a society, we remain painfully ill-equipped to manage this growing epidemic.

Every family touched by alcoholism carries its own set of stories—stories that often reveal the burdens placed on children far too young to bear them. Sometimes these stories are heart-wrenching, illustrating how roles of responsibility and care fall on young shoulders when parents are unable to manage their own lives.

Recently, a good friend from my golf league, who is also in his 70s, shared a personal story with me that struck a chord. It was particularly resonant for me, as I grew up in a family where my paternal grandfather was a dairy farmer. My friend recounted how, as a young boy, he took on far more than any child should have been asked to manage, all due to his father's drinking problem. The farm became both his sanctuary and his burden—a place where he learned resilience but also a place where he lost his childhood.

Hearing stories like his makes me reflect on how common it is for addiction to distort the natural order of things. Children grow up too quickly, stepping in to hold together what's left of a family. These experiences leave deep emotional scars, ones that many of us carry into adulthood and that often resurface when we face our own battles with addiction.

We are not alone in this. We've all seen, heard, or lived through similar stories. This is why community, sharing, and acknowledging our pasts are critical to recovery. It's through hearing one another's experiences that we gain perspective, strength, and, most importantly, hope. It's how we learn that while the weight of our pasts may feel heavy, we don't have to carry it alone.

My friend's story paints a vivid picture of what too many children of alcoholic parents endure. As a nine-year-old boy growing up in western Wisconsin, with two alcoholic parents, his childhood was anything but typical. His family owned a small dairy farm, and anyone familiar with dairy farming knows that the single most important task is making sure the cows are milked on time, twice a day, every single day. When cows aren't milked, they begin mooing loudly and relentlessly—there are no breaks, no vacations from this responsibility.

His parents, both active alcoholics, frequently left the farm to "run errands" in town, but these trips would often end with them at the bar. Time and time again, they'd lose track of time and not come home in time for the evening milking.

At just nine years old, my friend was forced to learn a hard lesson—if he didn't milk the cows himself before bed, he would inevitably be woken up in the middle of the night by his parents, drunk and angry, demanding he go out to the barn and help with the milking. After enough nights of disrupted sleep, he realized it was easier to just do it himself—tackling the burden of milking over 20 cows alone.

This story isn't just about the hard labor a child shouldn't have to shoulder; it's a reflection of the emotional and psychological toll alcoholism takes on families. The adults in his life were absent when they were most needed, and he learned far too early that he couldn't rely on them. The burden of responsibility fell squarely on his young shoulders.

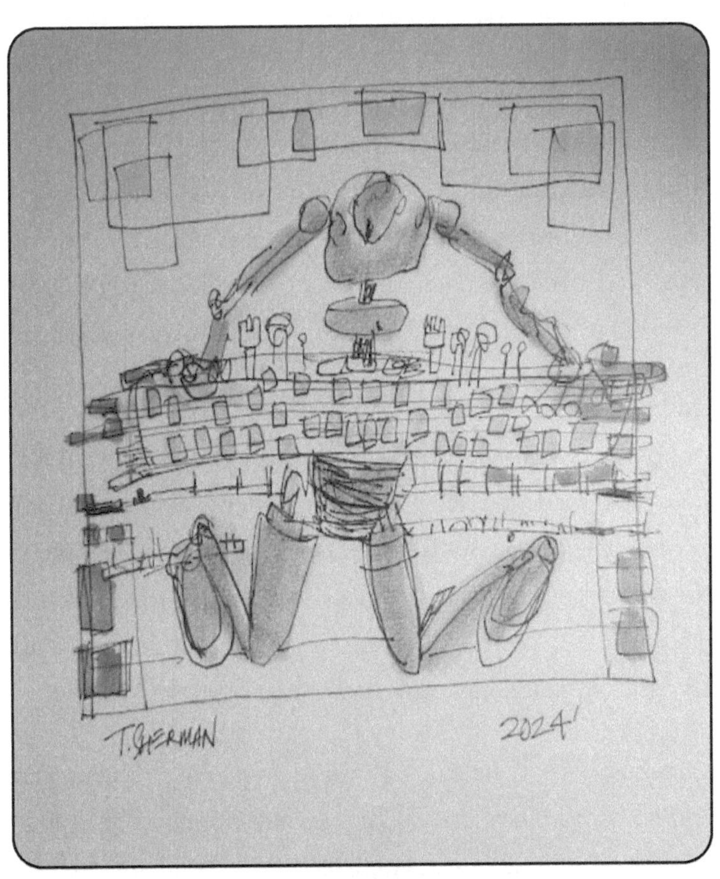

The emotional cost of growing up with alcoholic parents goes beyond the physical exhaustion of taking care of the farm. It creates a cycle of fear, anxiety, and a constant need for vigilance. This experience is not uncommon for the children of alcoholics—many are thrust into roles far beyond their years, forced to pick up the pieces left behind by addicted parents.

For my friend, this was just one story among many, but it illustrates a larger truth: the harmful behaviors of alcoholics ripple outwards, often landing hardest on those least equipped to handle them. The impact of these experiences follows children into adulthood, shaping their lives in profound ways. In many cases, it's these early burdens that lead to their own struggles with addiction, or it manifests in other ways, such as anxiety or depression.

Hearing stories like these is crucial for those of us in recovery. They remind us that addiction is not just an individual struggle—it affects families, communities, and future generations. By sharing our experiences, we offer strength and hope, showing that while the past may have shaped us, it doesn't have to define our future.

My friend's experience goes beyond the boundaries of physical cruelty or overt abuse, but the emotional toll of growing up in an alcoholic household had lasting effects on him and his younger sister, who also later became an alcoholic. This story highlights the invisible but powerful impact of emotional neglect. It's clear that family influence plays a significant role in shaping our tendencies toward addiction, and this case illustrates just how early those patterns begin.

Emotional neglect, while not as visible as physical abuse, can have profound consequences on a child's development, affecting their emotional and psychological well-being. It is characterized by a consistent lack of emotional support, validation, and responsiveness from caregivers, leaving the child feeling unseen and unimportant. Over time, this neglect can lead to a deep sense of unworthiness and emotional emptiness. For many, this void becomes fertile ground for addiction.

In households where emotional neglect is prevalent, the absence of emotional nurturing can stunt the development of healthy coping mechanisms. Children raised in these environments often struggle to handle stress, disappointment, or trauma because they've never learned how to manage these emotions in a healthy way. Instead, they might turn to external substances like alcohol or drugs as a way to numb the pain, fill the emotional void, or cope with life's inevitable hardships.

Unlike overt abuse, emotional neglect can be subtle and difficult to recognize, even for the person experiencing it. It might not involve shouting or violence, but the impact is just as real. Children growing up in these environments can feel invisible or like they don't matter. This lack of acknowledgment or emotional connection from their caregivers often leads them to question their self-worth. These feelings don't just go away as they grow older; they linger, often manifesting in anxiety, depression, or a deep-seated need to seek validation and comfort through unhealthy means.

In my friend's case, the emotional neglect from his parents not only forced him into premature adulthood, as he shouldered the responsibility of milking the cows when they failed to show up, but it also robbed him of the safety and security that children need to develop a healthy sense of self. The burdens placed on him, and later on his sister, represent just one of the many ways alcoholic behaviors trickle down to affect the youngest members of a family.

It's stories like these that show how important it is to acknowledge emotional neglect as a critical factor in addiction. Recognizing the signs of emotional neglect in ourselves and others is a first step toward healing. Emotional neglect may not leave visible scars, but the wounds run deep, and understanding this can help us foster empathy and compassion for those who have experienced it.

By sharing stories like these, we open up space for others to reflect on their own experiences, providing strength and hope to those in recovery. It also reminds us that while the past may shape us, we have the power to change the future.

Children who experience emotional neglect often struggle with self-esteem issues and a pervasive sense of loneliness. As they grow into adulthood, these unresolved feelings can drive them to seek solace in substances or behaviors that offer temporary relief or fulfillment. This is particularly common in those with addictive personalities, who often exhibit traits such as impulsivity, difficulty regulating emotions, and a tendency to escape reality—patterns frequently rooted in a history of emotional neglect.

The absence of healthy emotional connections during formative years leaves individuals vulnerable. They may search for external validation or relief, turning to alcohol, drugs, or compulsive behaviors like gambling or overeating in an attempt to fill the void. However, these behaviors are misguided attempts to cope, and they often entrench individuals deeper in cycles of shame and isolation, perpetuating their addiction. The temporary relief they find only masks the unresolved pain, creating a cycle that becomes increasingly difficult to escape.

The long-term effects of emotional neglect are profound. The lack of nurturing during childhood hinders emotional growth, leaving individuals ill-equipped to handle stress, disappointment, or trauma. This deficiency manifests in adulthood as difficulties in personal and professional development, strained relationships, and ongoing struggles with mental health issues such as anxiety, depression, and, ultimately, addiction.

Recovery from addiction often involves addressing not just the addictive behaviors but also the emotional wounds caused by neglect. Therapeutic approaches such as trauma-informed care and attachment-based therapies are essential in helping individuals heal. These therapies focus on building emotional resilience by acknowledging the deep-rooted pain and fostering self-awareness. Through these practices, individuals can develop healthier coping mechanisms and begin to break the cycle of addiction.

Moreover, the road to recovery is not just about overcoming addiction; it's about reclaiming one's emotional life. For many, this process involves re-learning how to form meaningful connections, both with others and with oneself. Building a support system and cultivating relationships that foster emotional growth and resilience are essential steps toward lasting recovery.

The importance of addressing emotional neglect as part of the addiction recovery process cannot be overstated. Recognizing and healing the emotional scars left by neglect allows individuals to step out of the shadow of their past and into a future filled with healthier coping strategies, greater emotional awareness, and, most importantly, the ability to form supportive, fulfilling relationships.

In essence, breaking free from addiction involves more than just overcoming the substance or behavior—it requires nurturing the emotional wounds that fed the addiction in the first place. By focusing on healing the emotional self, those in recovery can move toward a life of genuine fulfillment, free from the chains of both addiction and emotional neglect.

Emotional neglect is a key factor in the development of addictive personalities, as the absence of emotional support and validation can leave individuals searching for external sources of comfort. This need for solace often manifests in harmful addictions. Understanding this connection between emotional neglect and addiction is crucial for effective intervention and recovery. Addressing both the addiction itself and the emotional scars left by neglect is essential to lasting sobriety.

Healing from emotional neglect opens the door to healthier coping mechanisms and a more fulfilling life. However, recognizing and addressing these emotional wounds requires courage and a willingness to confront past trauma. This process is vital not only for personal recovery but for breaking the generational cycle of addiction and emotional neglect that so often plagues families.

Historically, society's efforts to address alcohol addiction have not always been successful. Prohibition, America's "great experiment" aimed at ending the nation's drinking problem, was a notable failure. It was abandoned in 1933, just six months before Alcoholics Anonymous was published. Prohibition was the result of over 50 years of lobbying by the powerful Temperance Movement, which firmly believed that banning alcohol would solve society's issues with drinking. Yet, the experiment proved disastrous, leading to more harm than good, as people found ways around the law or turned to more dangerous alternatives.

The founders of *Alcoholics Anonymous* were acutely aware of Prohibition's failure. The *Big Book*—AA's foundational text—frequently contrasts the society-wide failure of Prohibition with AA's focus on addressing the individual alcoholic's problem, not legislating society's drinking habits. This distinction was critical. AA wasn't about controlling everyone's alcohol consumption; it was about helping individuals who wanted to stop drinking. The founders, having lived through the temperance movement, knew that personal change, not political solutions, was the real path to recovery.

The personal stories of those who struggled with alcohol addiction, like the many tales shared in AA meetings, provide strength and hope for others. These stories serve as powerful reminders of the cunning, baffling, and patient nature of addiction. They highlight the importance of addressing the internal emotional and psychological struggles that often accompany addiction. The real change comes from within, from confronting not just the addiction but also the emotional pain and neglect that fuel it.

In the end, recovery is not just about abstaining from alcohol or drugs; it's about emotional healing. Therapy, mindfulness, and community support all play significant roles in helping individuals rebuild their lives. By focusing on the underlying emotional wounds and not just the symptoms of addiction, we can help people reclaim their lives, strengthen their relationships, and find peace in sobriety.

This revision adds more emotional depth to the content, emphasizing the importance of addressing the emotional scars from neglect and focusing on both the personal and societal lessons learned from history. The tone is more intimate and reflective, allowing readers to connect more deeply with the message while maintaining the essential points.

Nearly 100 years ago, in Dayton, Ohio, a group of white professional men began gathering to discuss their struggles with alcohol. Though not affiliated with any religious group directly, most of these men were members of The Oxford Group, a non-denominational Protestant Christian organization. These early meetings would influence the eventual formation of Alcoholics Anonymous (AA), whose roots are deeply intertwined with spiritual principles.

During this time, America had just witnessed the failure of Prohibition, a nationwide experiment that sought to eradicate alcohol consumption by making it illegal. Prohibition, which ended in 1933, was backed by over 50 years of political lobbying from the powerful Temperance Movement. While well-intentioned, this movement failed to address the complexities of individual alcohol addiction. The creators of AA knew that prohibition had only addressed the societal aspect of alcohol, but it had done little to help individuals struggling with the disease of alcoholism.

Alcoholics Anonymous, first published in 1939, sought to offer a new, more personal solution. The *Big Book*, as it's called, clearly states that its mission is to help the individual alcoholic, not to legislate anyone's drinking. AA founders Bill Wilson and Dr. Bob Smith, who both had extensive involvement with The Oxford Group, knew from experience that tackling alcoholism required spiritual and moral transformation, not governmental regulation.

The Oxford Group, founded in 1921 by Frank Buchman as "A First Century Christian Fellowship," had a profound influence on AA's structure and guiding principles. Bill Wilson himself acknowledged this, stating that early AA derived its concepts of self-examination, acknowledging character defects, making amends, and helping others directly from The Oxford Group. The group emphasized personal moral and spiritual change as a pathway to a better life and, by extension, a better society.

The teachings of The Oxford Group were centered around what they called the Four Absolutes: honesty, purity, unselfishness, and love. Members were encouraged to engage in practices like self-examination, confession, restitution for harm done, and living these values daily. These principles laid the foundation for AA's Twelve Steps, which encourage a similar path of moral and spiritual awakening.

Understanding this history highlights the spiritual and community-based nature of recovery. It shows that AA is not just a set of tools to stop drinking but a way to transform one's entire life. The emphasis on individual responsibility, moral inventory, and helping others is what makes AA unique in its approach. It's a reminder that recovery is a deeply personal journey, supported by a community of others who have walked the same path.

This group of men, all successful businessmen with families, had spent years grappling with their increasing reliance on alcohol. Their lives, once stable, had gradually begun to unravel, and they were left confused and overwhelmed. For most of them, drinking had been a part of their lives for over a decade, but the consequences were catching up. As their family lives and careers began to collapse, they turned to each other for support, hoping that by coming together, they could make sense of their shared struggles.

In those early meetings, they created a space for honesty, openness, and mutual aid. This support network would form the bedrock of Alcoholics Anonymous, and its emphasis on shared experience and vulnerability remains central to AA's mission today. The group's efforts reflected a deep desire not just to stop drinking but to rebuild their lives and relationships.

One of the most influential forces in the formation of AA was The Oxford Group, a Christian fellowship that emphasized personal moral transformation as a path to societal change. The Oxford Group had a profound effect on the founding members of AA, including Bill Wilson and Dr. Bob Smith, who drew on its spiritual principles to form the basis of AA's approach. Bill Wilson credited The Oxford Group with shaping much of AA's philosophy, particularly its focus on self-examination, acknowledging character defects, making amends, and helping others.

The influence of The Oxford Group is also evident in AA's understanding of a Higher Power, or God, as central to the recovery process. This spiritual focus continues to guide AA today, offering members the opportunity to connect with something greater than themselves in their pursuit of sobriety. The group's emphasis on individual moral change also inspired AA's commitment to personal accountability, rather than legislating drinking for society as a whole—a lesson learned from the failure of Prohibition.

Prohibition, America's attempt to solve the "alcohol problem" through legal measures, had been a resounding failure. Its end in 1933, just a few years before the founding of AA, reinforced the belief that alcoholism was not a societal issue that could be fixed with laws, but a deeply personal one. The Oxford Group's approach, with its focus on personal transformation and moral responsibility, offered a new way forward.

The group's influence extended beyond AA's spiritual elements. The Oxford Group's focus on staying out of politics and instead focusing on individual change also shaped AA's philosophy. This avoidance of political entanglement allowed AA to remain inclusive and focused on its primary goal: helping individuals achieve and maintain sobriety. This emphasis on personal moral transformation, mutual support, and spiritual growth would become the foundation upon which AA was built, and it continues to serve as a guiding force for the millions of people who have found recovery through its programs.

The Oxford Group may not have explicitly championed pacifism, but its core values—nonviolence, reconciliation, and personal moral transformation—reflect a spirit of peace and nonviolent conflict resolution. Members of the group were urged to seek peaceful resolutions and strive for a just, harmonious world through individual change. This approach naturally aligned with pacifist principles, encouraging members to be peacemakers within their communities. The Group's emphasis on inner transformation as a foundation for broader social change laid the groundwork for a culture of nonviolence, even if it wasn't overtly defined as such.

Although the Oxford Group's influence has faded with time, its foundational teachings continue to resonate within Alcoholics Anonymous and similar recovery movements. AA adopted the Oxford Group's reliance on a Higher Power, a significant pillar of its approach. This concept of surrendering to a Higher Power helps individuals find peace with their struggles and make room for healing—a spiritual realignment that is both personal and profound.

Central practices, such as self-examination and the taking of a moral inventory, became cornerstones in both groups, stressing the importance of introspection for lasting change. The concept of admitting wrongs to oneself, to a Higher Power, and to others is echoed in AA's approach, mirroring the Oxford Group's commitment to humility and transparency. This moral inventory—paired with making amends for past wrongs—encourages recovery not only from addiction but also from the emotional and moral injuries that accompany it.

The Oxford Group's emphasis on sharing experiences and aiding others is likewise embedded in AA's culture, evident in its service-focused 12-step model. These foundational principles helped shape AA into a global movement rooted in spiritual growth, shared experience, and community support, empowering individuals to find recovery in unity and strength.

These early meetings would eventually give birth to Alcoholics Anonymous, a testament to the profound impact of the Oxford Group's values. The commitment to inner transformation, service, and community spirit remains at the heart of AA's approach, creating a legacy that continues to inspire hope and recovery today.

At the heart of AA's spiritual framework lies a reliance on a Higher Power for personal change, an approach directly inherited from the Oxford Group. This reliance encourages individuals to seek strength beyond themselves, anchoring them in a process of spiritual growth that is critical in recovery. The Oxford Group's emphasis on self-examination and moral inventory became pivotal practices in AA, allowing individuals to confront their character flaws and past actions with humility and honesty.

Central to both organizations is the process of admitting wrongs—to oneself, to God, and to others—a step that fosters personal accountability. By integrating the concept of making amends, AA encourages individuals to face past harms, transforming guilt and regret into opportunities for healing. This influence of moral accountability is foundational, creating a recovery pathway that encompasses more than just sobriety; it emphasizes moral and spiritual repair.

The Oxford Group's focus on sharing experiences and offering support to others has also become integral to AA's philosophy. This sense of mutual aid, of one person reaching out to help another, is a cornerstone of AA's community-driven recovery approach. These early spiritual teachings continue to resonate within AA and have influenced countless other recovery programs, making the Oxford Group's legacy one of enduring relevance in the fight against addiction. Through these principles, AA has not only provided tools for sobriety but has also promoted a pathway to emotional and spiritual renewal, one member at a time.

The Oxford Group encouraged members to openly share experiences and support each other—a concept that became central to Alcoholics Anonymous (AA) through its principle of service. These early gatherings planted the seeds for AA's foundation, which has since evolved into a global recovery movement focused on both spiritual growth and community support.

The spiritual philosophy of AA and its 12-step model, which promote reliance on a Higher Power and personal accountability, largely stems from the Oxford Group's teachings. This approach emphasized that by admitting personal wrongs, making amends, and supporting others, members could cultivate a life of purpose and moral integrity. As AA grew, it became a foundational model for addiction recovery, setting a new standard for treatment that continues to influence countless programs today.

While the earliest AA members were predominantly white businessmen, the fellowship has expanded widely over the decades to serve diverse populations. Addiction affects people of all backgrounds, and AA's principles of empathy, openness, and resilience have proved universally applicable. Today, nearly all treatment programs draw from AA's core concepts—mutual aid, shared experience, and spiritual support—though these may be adapted to address not only alcoholism but a wide array of substance and behavioral addictions. The inclusive evolution of AA reflects a profound understanding: while experiences and substances may differ, the roots of addiction share common ground.

As addiction has evolved into a widespread societal challenge, we've come to realize that alcoholism is just one facet of the issue. Entire families, communities, and even cultures have been profoundly impacted by various forms of addiction, which now include drugs, gambling, and compulsive behaviors. AA, initially formed with a singular focus on alcohol, laid the groundwork for addressing addiction through shared experience, emotional support, and spiritual growth. Over time, it became evident that many principles fundamental to AA's success could be applied to other addictions as well.

The success of AA inspired a multitude of 12-step programs, such as Narcotics Anonymous, Al-Anon, and Gamblers Anonymous, each addressing different forms of addiction. These programs maintain AA's foundational values: fellowship, shared struggles, and unwavering support, highlighting that recovery is not a solitary journey.

This broadened approach reflects a powerful truth: at the core, addiction often stems from similar underlying pain. AA's model has fostered an inclusive community, not just for alcoholics but for individuals facing diverse addictive behaviors, showing that the roots of addiction—whether alcohol, narcotics, or gambling—share much in common.

CHAPTER THREE

DEFENSIVE COORDINATOR: DEFENDING THE ENTIRE FIELD

IN RECENT DECADES, ADDICTION HAS INCREASINGLY BEEN recognized as a disease rather than a moral failing. This shift has broadened conversations around recovery, making room for an inclusive approach that acknowledges various forms of addiction and the complex struggles that accompany them. Advances in research and mental health have illuminated the intricate nature of addiction, prompting AA and similar organizations to adapt and include other substance dependencies and compulsive behaviors.

This evolution has given rise to new recovery programs that build upon AA's foundation. What began as a fellowship focused exclusively on alcoholism has grown into a global support network that addresses a wide spectrum of addictions. Programs like Narcotics Anonymous and Gamblers Anonymous reflect the expansion of AA's original principles, embracing the shared experiences and communal support that have always been at AA's core. Despite debates among different addiction groups about similarities and differences in approach, AA's model continues to demonstrate that, at the root, addiction is a common struggle, requiring both individual transformation and collective resilience.

Interestingly, AA's choice to grant autonomy to individual groups has allowed the program to adapt while remaining accessible and effective across diverse backgrounds and experiences. Alcoholics can be a tough crowd to coach; many of us are strong-willed, fiercely opinionated, and resistant to change—qualities that addiction itself can amplify. But the reality is that addiction doesn't discriminate, and neither should the approach to treating it.

The journey to recovery often begins with a moment of reckoning. For me, it was the 1984 arrest for drunk driving. After spending 30 days in an inpatient treatment center—my court-mandated introduction to Alcoholics Anonymous—I confronted a possibility that had never crossed my mind: I might be an alcoholic. I told the young prosecutor handling my case as much. His response was one of surprise; no one in his experience had admitted a lack of control over alcohol before. Apparently, I was his first "real" alcoholic.

I had lived my entire life in an environment steeped in alcohol, oblivious to the notion of addiction or that it could even be treated. My mind was caught in a spiral, not on my job or family but on the after-work hours

I eagerly anticipated. Time with my family felt like an afterthought; it was my regular nights out at the "Time Out Bar" that dominated my thoughts. My life had become about anticipating that next drink, more than the people or moments that should have mattered most.

It's this power that addiction wields—drawing us away from what we hold dear, one drink, one night at a time. This truth is universal, no matter the substance or behavior. Recovery is not just about abstaining from a drink; it's about reconnecting with life itself, rebuilding the bonds we neglected, and addressing the deep-seated issues we've long ignored.

AA showed me a path, illuminating both the disease and the promise of recovery. And while each of our paths may be unique, the foundation remains the same. We admit our powerlessness over addiction and lean into a community built on shared experience, mutual support, and an unwavering commitment to change.

In those days, everything I looked forward to had alcohol at its center. It was a time when law enforcement often turned a blind eye, especially if you had status in the community. Professional people didn't go to jail. Instead, they might get a warning or an escort home. "One for the road" wasn't just an expression; it was a literal last drink, taken in the car while driving to the next destination. In northern Michigan, open intoxicants weren't questioned, accepted as casually as not wearing a seatbelt, long before such safety laws were in place.

This culture wasn't just permissive—it enabled denial. Court-ordered sobriety measures, like mandatory testing and attendance at Alcoholics Anonymous meetings, became routine but often ineffective barriers. At nearly every AA meeting, you'd find people lining up after the meeting, not for the fellowship but to get their court-ordered attendance slips signed. It was clear that simply showing up wasn't going to cut through the deeply ingrained patterns or attitudes toward alcohol.

The journey to sobriety, real sobriety, doesn't come from attendance slips or forced abstinence. It begins with a conscious choice to confront the hold addiction has on us. It wasn't the law or the threats of punishment that eventually guided me to change—it was understanding that I could no longer ignore the destructive path I was on.

Despite its best intentions, forced sobriety through the legal system remains an imperfect solution. The requirement to attend AA meetings or submit to daily testing doesn't change the core challenge: sobriety can't be imposed from the outside. It's a choice that has to be made within. Yet, these legal mandates have become standard tools in the fight against addiction, even as we see alarming statistics of repeat offenders who continue to cycle through the system.

Losing a driver's license after a DUI rarely stops people from getting behind the wheel again. For many, the addiction's pull is simply stronger than any consequence, as proven by the rising number of repeat offenses. Courts and law enforcement know this too well. Officers can tell stories of the same faces and names, the same violations, and the same empty promises. There's a tragic irony here: we ask the legal system to enforce sobriety, yet those mandates often become just another hurdle, one easily evaded for the addict who hasn't yet chosen recovery.

I've witnessed firsthand how friends and former teammates struggled with mandated sobriety. A close friend, despite multiple violations, spent months in county jail. But the very day he was released, his son found him on the front porch, drinking a beer, flipping through the mail. Addiction, it seems, has a powerful way of waiting for us.

In this culture of "forced recovery," we often miss the heart of the problem: addiction isn't about the substance alone but the underlying void it's meant to fill. And while the court-mandated attendance at AA might look like a hopeful step, without a real willingness to face that void, it's a hollow gesture. True recovery is about so much more than showing up—it's about choosing to change.

Forced sobriety can be a stopgap, but it rarely delivers lasting results. Court officers must understand its limitations, especially given the way addiction can lay dormant, waiting for an opportunity to resurface. Sobriety needs to be a choice, one fueled by a genuine desire for change, rather than something imposed by a mandate.

Last year, I had an experience that underscored this truth. I was out in my front yard, playing with Fern, my daughter's yellow Labrador, and Atticus, my black Lab. Fern—true to her gentle, friendly nature—gave an enthusiastic bark when a familiar neighbor passed by with his small dog. This neighbor, with a track record of arrests for disorderly conduct and drunk driving, reacted instantly. Dropping his dog's leash, he charged toward us, shouting and cursing as he tried to kick Fern.

In a flash, his startled little dog bolted, heading for home. I quickly called Fern back, whistling to calm her, feeling the tension of the moment. This man's unhinged reaction spoke volumes about the fragile nature of forced sobriety—an exterior shell with a storm just below the surface.

Forced sobriety, like my neighbor's volatile state, often masks the underlying issues that keep addiction alive. It's a temporary fix that fails to address the emotional and psychological roots of dependency. And while it may offer temporary compliance, it rarely nurtures the lasting change that comes from within.

I had barely taken a step down my driveway when I spotted him—my neighbor, eyes wild, words slurred, and fists clenched. I shouted, frustration and self-preservation mingling in my voice. But in an instant, his demeanor shifted. Without warning, he stormed up the driveway, aiming to tackle me. Years of wrestling coaching instincts kicked in, and I squared myself, bracing against his weight.

He was younger, taller, and packed over 300 pounds. He lunged, fists drawn back, but I was ready, blocking his swing. After a moment, he backed off, cursing under his breath as he trudged back down, his dog already trotting home. I'd had the experience to defend myself, but that encounter left me shaken.

When I called the county sheriff, a deputy came out, took my statement, studied the tracks in the snow, and went to his house. Minutes later, I watched as they led him out in cuffs—a temporary end to a cycle that was just beginning.

That night set off a year of courtroom visits and county jail stints, meetings with the prosecutor, bail jumps, failed sobriety tests, and short releases. Every brief reprieve seemed to drag us both deeper into this powerless web of addiction. In the end, he chose jail over parole with daily testing, a common choice for those who prefer a short term behind bars over long, uncertain days under surveillance. It's a tough decision, one rooted in the feeling that life has spun beyond control.

Addiction doesn't just affect one person—it stretches like a shadow over family, friends, and even neighbors. For a while, a person might stay sober for their family, become what we call a "dry drunk." But without a real commitment, it's only a matter of time. And codependents, just like the addicts they support, suffer in their own way unless they, too, understand the depths of addiction.

Joe Namath once shared that he'd spent the first thirteen years of his recovery just holding on, "white-knuckling" through each day as a so-called "dry drunk." He was technically sober, but peace remained out of reach. I understood that story all too well—only, in my case, it took even longer to get there. I had stopped drinking, but I wasn't happy. Life was just…empty, a hollow attempt at survival without the real freedom that sobriety promised. My addiction had simply shifted, lurking beneath the surface, waiting for another outlet.

For me, the real confrontation with my addiction came not in a bar but at a blackjack table. It was there that I began to understand the root of my struggle—an addiction that went beyond substances and instead burrowed into my very nature. Facing that "tap root" of my addiction, I realized that I needed more than just willpower. I needed to confront the underlying drives that had held me captive for so long, and, perhaps for the first time, I was ready to dig deep.

Recovery isn't about abstaining alone; it's about finding peace within that abstinence. It's about truly living—not just avoiding. And that requires an inner journey to the core of what drives us to escape, a journey that is made stronger and more bearable when shared with others who know the path.

The story of the Washingtonian Temperance Society offers an early chapter in the journey of recovery—a history rooted in resilience and a deep understanding of addiction. Founded in 1840 in Baltimore,

Maryland, during a time when alcoholism ran rampant across the United States, this movement was not born from the pulpit or lofty ideals but from the grit of working-class men who had lived through the worst of alcohol's devastation. Like so many today, they knew the isolating grip of addiction firsthand and understood that healing would require more than good intentions; it would require a community.

Named after George Washington, a symbol of integrity, the Washingtonian Society took a different path from the well-meaning temperance movements led by the middle and upper classes. This was a grassroots movement, founded by men who needed each other's stories, support, and accountability to confront their addiction. They didn't preach abstinence as an ideal but offered a safe space to share their failures and triumphs without judgment. By grounding themselves in personal testimony, they reshaped the way society viewed alcoholism— not as a moral failing but as a human struggle shared by all.

Their meetings resonated because they were real, honest, and full of empathy. Stories of men who had once lost everything now offering their arms to lift up others gave the movement a unique power. As it grew, the Washingtonian Temperance Society began to draw thousands, shifting the narrative on addiction by demonstrating that recovery wasn't a solo journey. It was a collective effort, a "team sport" long before that language was ever used.

The Society's legacy didn't end in the 19th century; it set the stage for organizations like Alcoholics Anonymous and the Women's Christian Temperance Union. The idea that addiction could be met with mutual support, that one person's story could serve as a lifeline for another, continues to be central to modern recovery programs.

By grounding the discussion of addiction within a community, the Washingtonians highlighted that recovery is possible when we come together, lifting one another up. This foundational shift—seeing addiction as a collective issue rather than a personal flaw—helped remove the stigma and offered a new perspective on sobriety that still endures. Today, we honor this history by recognizing that every recovery journey is built on shared stories, understanding, and a commitment to face our battles together.

Women have long been on the front lines of the fight against alcohol dependency. As early as the 19th century, they rose to the challenge in movements like the Women's Christian Temperance Union, established in 1874. In those days, alcoholism was tearing families apart, creating a crisis that left women to pick up the pieces. They organized, marched, and advocated, determined to address the social harm caused by alcohol. This commitment became the bedrock of their role in addiction recovery—a role that has only deepened over time.

As the field of addiction treatment evolved in the 20th century, women continued breaking new ground. No longer limited to advocacy alone, they stepped into positions as counselors, healthcare providers, and recovery advocates, bringing unique insight to the process. When Alcoholics Anonymous was founded in 1935, women, though underrepresented, began participating in the program. Their inclusion helped spotlight the need for a more personal approach to recovery—one that acknowledged the diverse ways addiction affected men and women alike.

Over the years, society has come to recognize that women experience addiction differently and face unique challenges in recovery. As this awareness grew, so did the need for gender-specific approaches, and by the late 20th century, dedicated programs emerged to support women navigating sobriety. These specialized resources offered not only treatment but also understanding—a safe space to explore the emotional roots of addiction and build strength through shared experiences.

Today, women are integral to all facets of alcohol treatment, from providing peer support to holding leadership roles within treatment facilities. Their journey has transformed the field, showing that recovery isn't just a fight against addiction but a collective effort to restore lives and rebuild communities. This is the legacy women bring to the table: resilience, empathy, and the conviction that sobriety is, at its core, a team effort.

When I was arrested in 1984, I didn't know anything about alcoholism—no one really did, at least not in a way that made sense. I was part of a society that had no language or framework for what we now recognize as addiction. To us, alcoholism was a vague notion, something we knew by sight but never by understanding. It took entering a hospital treatment center for me to even begin grasping the concept of what alcoholism really was.

Back then, it was just Uncle Joe who drank too much, who turned louder and happier, or maybe angrier than the rest. In the media, alcoholics were often caricatures—the "town drunk," a punchline or an oddball in movies, like Otis in *The Andy Griffith Show*, with his self-imposed visits to the jail cell. We didn't question why these characters drank or why they might reach for a bottle in a moment of pain or frustration. We laughed and moved on, our understanding thin and dismissive.

The real impact of alcoholism, though, was harder to ignore for those who lived with it. People learned to keep their heads down, to quietly endure, because there was no real support. Silence was the norm, and those who suffered bore it alone.

Entering treatment changed all that for me. I was suddenly forced to confront the reality I'd been living in, to see alcoholism not as a quirky personality trait but as a profound, life-altering illness. And as I looked around, I realized I wasn't alone. My story, once isolating, was now a shared experience. That realization was powerful—it was the beginning of understanding that recovery is not a solitary fight but a journey made possible by community, honesty, and shared strength.

Desire and craving might seem similar, but they're worlds apart—distinct psychological states that, for some, never become intertwined. Understanding the difference between them is key, and for many of us, this understanding is part of what sets the journey to recovery in motion.

Desire is natural and can be as simple as wanting something good in our lives. It can motivate us to set goals, pursue dreams, or find joy. In its best form, desire pushes us toward fulfillment and growth. Craving, though—that's another story. Craving is desire gone rogue, a hunger that takes on a life of its own, often hidden just beneath the surface until it's too intense to ignore. It grips us, overrides our intentions, and whispers that we're powerless without the very thing that holds us captive. For some, cravings are so embedded that they feel inseparable from who we are, lurking just out of sight yet steering us in ways we don't always understand.

I think back to childhood, that time when most of us learn the meaning of "no" and the boundaries it implies. The "terrible twos" are famous for this—tiny personalities testing limits, learning to process frustration and the denial of a want. By age five or six, most children have a sense of boundaries, but for some of us, those lessons never quite took hold. For reasons beyond our control, some of us didn't learn to sit with the "no," and it's easy to see now how that gap might have fed the addictive personalities we grew into.

Our early struggles with cravings may have started innocently enough, but over time, they became more than just passing wants. They became an ache, a relentless drive that defined our choices and blurred the lines between healthy desire and overpowering need. In recovery, understanding this difference—where desire ends, and craving begins—is a vital step toward breaking free.

We alcoholics can be a stubborn bunch; no denying that. It's often said that the most hard-headed people on Earth have found their way to recovery meetings, and that feels about right. The way we handle desire can start from such a young age that some argue it might be genetic. Whether addiction is in our genes or rooted in our experiences, it's a complex question I'll leave to the experts. Truthfully, that debate doesn't make much difference when you're in the middle of it, fighting to find your way to sobriety. For those of us trying to stay sober, knowing exactly where it all began doesn't change the work we have to do today.

In the end, no gene has ever been pinpointed as the cause of alcoholism. What we do know is that the paths we walk and the battles we face often look similar. The "disease" label serves as a reminder of the challenges we face and the fact that it's a condition requiring ongoing care. Whether we're predisposed by nature, shaped by nurture, or both, the goal remains the same: to find a way out, to break the cycle, and to live a life that's ours again.

Sobriety requires that we look beyond where the battle started and focus on where we want to go. Our stubbornness, if anything, can be our strength—a willingness to fight through the hardest moments, find support, and keep moving forward.

Alcohol use disorder can sometimes be tied to certain personality traits, though having these traits doesn't mean someone is destined to struggle with alcohol. Still, recognizing these patterns can be enlightening for those of us on the path to sobriety. Here are a few personality traits often associated with alcoholism:

1. **Impulsivity**: A tendency to jump into things without much thought. This trait can make it easy to reach for a drink before considering the impact, leading to risky behavior and, sometimes, regrets the morning after.

2. **Low self-esteem**: Struggling with feelings of inadequacy or worthlessness. Alcohol might feel like a way to quiet those negative thoughts, offering a temporary sense of comfort that eventually becomes a cycle of dependency.

3. **High stress tolerance**: Many of us pride ourselves on handling stress, even if that means burying it deep. Drinking can seem like a quick fix for stress or emotional pain—an easy "out" that, over time, becomes harder to resist.

4. **Social anxiety**: That unease in social settings is all too common. For some, alcohol acts like a social crutch, making it easier to feel "normal" around others, even if the relief is fleeting.

5. **Low conscientiousness**: When we're less detail-oriented or mindful of our actions, it's easier to fall into habits without thinking much about their consequences, including drinking.

6. **Emotional instability**: Intense feelings or mood swings can be overwhelming. For those of us who find it difficult to manage emotions, alcohol might feel like a release valve, even if it complicates things in the long run.

7. **Rebelliousness**: Some of us have an inner urge to defy rules or authority. Drinking can start as a way to assert independence, a small rebellion, before we realize how much control it's taken from us.

Recognizing these traits in ourselves is a first step toward understanding how they might fuel our relationship with alcohol. Rather than seeing them as obstacles, we can view them as opportunities for growth, ways to explore healthier coping strategies and build resilience. In recovery, we learn to channel these parts of ourselves into positive actions, drawing strength from those who walk the path with us.

Impulsivity and low self-esteem can be common threads among those of us dealing with alcohol use disorder, each feeding into the other in ways that create a powerful cycle. Alcohol's effect on the brain is a big part of this. When we drink, it alters our brain chemistry, particularly with neurotransmitters like dopamine, which play a role in impulse control and reward. Drinking can feel like an easy fix for a bad day, but it's a fix that comes at a cost, leading us down a path where making impulsive choices becomes second nature.

It's not just about the chemical effects, though. Regular drinking has a way of dulling our sensitivity to the consequences. We might start by making a few poor decisions, and before long, those choices feel routine, the dangers masked by a sense of "normalcy." Social situations can add fuel to this fire. In settings where drinking is encouraged, the pressure to keep up or fit in makes it easier to make risky decisions without thinking. It feels like the alcohol gives us freedom, but it's a freedom that's temporary and often misleading.

For many of us, impulsivity also connects to deeper challenges. Conditions like ADHD or mood disorders can increase our impulsive tendencies, and alcohol might seem like a quick way to cope. But the relief is temporary. The cycle continues: impulsive choices lead to more drinking, which, in turn, leads to further impaired judgment. It's easy to get lost in it.

Then there's self-esteem. Many people struggling with alcohol use deal with low self-worth, carrying a heavy burden of guilt and shame over their drinking habits. That shame can slowly chip away at any confidence we once had, leaving us stuck, feeling unworthy of change. It's a hard place to be, feeling like we're not enough. But recognizing these patterns and understanding the cycle can be a powerful first step. Knowing the "why" behind these traits gives us a chance to break free—to reclaim our judgment, rebuild our self-worth, and find a healthier path forward.

Struggles with alcohol can chip away at self-esteem in ways that are hard to repair. Many of us end up seeing ourselves as failures, convinced we're too weak to control our behavior or meet our own expectations. This negative self-image often starts subtly, creeping in as we struggle to stay sober or manage the damage caused by drinking. As relationships suffer and we face feelings of isolation and rejection, the blow to our self-worth deepens. Each conflict, every disappointed friend or family member, becomes one more reminder of the ways we feel we're falling short.

For some, alcohol becomes a way to escape these feelings of inadequacy. It offers a break from the guilt, a temporary ease. But it's a fragile peace, and once the effects wear off, we're often left with even more reasons to feel low. This cycle—using alcohol to cope with low self-esteem, only to find that drinking drags us down further—is one of the toughest challenges in recovery. It's a loop that's hard to escape because each drink can feel like a brief answer to the pain, even though we know it will come back stronger.

Then there's the weight of stigma. Society's judgments about alcoholism can lead us to internalize shame and self-blame. It's exhausting, carrying not only the burden of the addiction itself but also the feeling that others see us as "less than" or as people who can't control themselves. This judgment can bleed into every part of our lives, holding us back from reaching personal and professional goals and reinforcing a sense of failure and unmet potential.

This complex relationship between alcohol and self-esteem can make recovery feel like a steep uphill climb. But recognizing how these pieces fit together is a step toward healing. In recovery, we learn that self-worth doesn't have to be tied to perfection or never slipping up again. Instead, we begin to rebuild, piece by piece, supported by a team that understands the struggle and knows that our worth goes deeper than any temporary failure.

High stress tolerance is a common trait among many of us who struggle with alcohol, but it's often a complex and misleading shield. Here are some of the ways this so-called "tolerance" can develop:

1. **Coping Mechanisms**: Some of us built up a tolerance to stress simply to survive. Life can throw tough situations at us, and over time, we learn to mask the pain. Alcohol can feel like a quick way to escape these stressors, leading us to believe we're handling things better than we are.

2. **Adaptation Over Time**: Chronic drinking changes our brain chemistry, making us approach stress differently. This adaptation can feel like resilience, but it often masks the true emotional strain, leaving underlying stress responses unresolved.

3. **Dissociation**: Alcohol can numb us, temporarily making everything seem less intense. This numbing effect tricks us into thinking we're handling stress well. But in reality, it's just creating an illusion of strength, one that fades when the alcohol wears off.

4. **Desensitization**: Constant exposure to stress, especially when paired with drinking, can desensitize us over time. What once felt overwhelming becomes familiar, not because we've mastered it, but because we've grown numb to it. It's a coping strategy, but not a healthy one.

5. **Social Environment**: Sometimes, we find ourselves in social circles where drinking is normalized as a way to "deal" with stress. This culture can create a false sense of high stress tolerance, as we follow the crowd rather than face our struggles head-on.

These factors often create a confusing relationship between alcohol and stress management. What seems like a high tolerance is often just a mask, and removing it can feel daunting. But recovery is about learning to face life with true resilience, without relying on the temporary shields we once used. Breaking this cycle is challenging, but with support, we begin to replace those false tolerances with real strength.

Social anxiety and alcohol use often go hand-in-hand, creating a cycle that's hard to break. For many of us, drinking can feel like a lifeline in social settings, offering temporary relief from anxiety. Here are some of the ways social anxiety and alcohol can feed off each other:

1. **Coping Strategy**: Alcohol can feel like an "easy fix" for social anxiety, helping to temporarily quiet those nerves and make us feel more comfortable. In the moment, a drink might feel like the confidence boost we need, even though it's only a band-aid solution.

2. **Fear of Judgment**: Many of us worry about how others see us, especially if we're struggling with alcohol use. That fear of being judged or misunderstood can amplify anxiety, making us even more hesitant to engage in social settings.

3. **Negative Experiences**: Embarrassing or difficult moments while drinking—things we regret or wish we could take back—can make social situations feel even more daunting. The thought of making another mistake, of facing another uncomfortable moment, can heighten our anxiety about being around others.

4. **Low Self-Esteem**: When we're carrying feelings of inadequacy or low self-worth, social anxiety often feels magnified. Facing others becomes harder because we're already questioning ourselves, doubting our worth before we've even walked into the room.

5. **Isolation**: Over time, chronic alcohol use can lead to isolation, making social situations feel foreign and overwhelming. The more we pull back from others, the more anxious we feel about reconnecting, creating a cycle of self-consciousness and withdrawal.

6. **Mental Health Issues**: Social anxiety doesn't usually stand alone. For many, it coexists with other mental health struggles like depression or generalized anxiety, and alcohol use can make these issues even more pronounced. Drinking might seem like a coping mechanism, but it often intensifies the very feelings we're trying to escape.

These factors create a complex relationship between social anxiety and alcohol use, where each one fuels the other. We may reach for a drink to ease the tension, but in the end, alcohol deepens the anxiety, making both recovery and social interactions even more challenging. Recognizing this cycle can be empowering—it's a step toward reclaiming control, finding healthier ways to face social situations, and learning to engage with others without needing the "crutch" of alcohol.

Chronic alcohol use can take a toll on our ability to think clearly, plan ahead, and make decisions that align with our values. Over time, alcohol can blur the line between what matters to us and what we feel compelled to do. The effects reach into our personal, professional, and social lives, as the urge to drink often overshadows other responsibilities. Many of us find ourselves struggling to follow through on plans, missing deadlines, or letting down the people we care about. It's not because we don't want to be there—it's because alcohol has a way of altering our priorities, sometimes without us even realizing it.

One of the biggest impacts alcohol has is on our emotional stability. It can make us impulsive, quick to react, and less likely to pause and think things through. The ability to weigh our actions against their consequences becomes harder to hold onto, and that diminished sense of foresight makes planning and organizing feel overwhelming. This lack of control over our choices can create a ripple effect, making us feel like we're constantly playing catch-up, trying to put out fires instead of moving forward with intention.

As our cognitive abilities take a hit, so does our sense of conscientiousness. With the focus on immediate relief, long-term goals and responsibilities begin to slip through the cracks. It's a gradual process, one that can make us feel like we're losing touch with who we are and what we value. Recognizing this shift is essential—it's a wake-up call that reminds us that recovery is about more than giving up alcohol; it's about reclaiming our ability to live purposefully, to make choices that reflect the lives we want to lead.

The physical toll of alcoholism unfolds gradually, yet it's relentless, impacting the body in ways that may not be obvious at first. For many of us, it begins with the need to drink more to feel the same effects—a pattern that only seems to grow stronger over time. As tolerance builds, so do the side effects. Hangovers become routine, sleep becomes elusive, and our digestion starts to suffer. The liver—the body's primary filter—begins to struggle, showing early signs of damage like fatty liver and inflammation. Memory becomes unreliable, and even simple tasks require more focus than they once did.

If drinking continues, the body's resilience wears thin. The liver takes the brunt, facing progressive damage like fibrosis and cirrhosis. The heart, too, becomes vulnerable, with high blood pressure, irregular heartbeats, and cardiomyopathy—each a potential risk. Everyday activities become harder as conditions like gastritis, ulcers, and pancreatitis develop. And then there's the nervous system: tremors, neuropathy, and cognitive decline creep in, making it harder to ignore the damage.

At its worst, cirrhosis can lead to liver failure, sometimes requiring a transplant as the only option. The damage often spreads, affecting the kidneys, heart, and brain, bringing on a range of other complications. Alcohol increases the risk of cancers, particularly in the liver, throat, and esophagus, adding another layer of risk to an already heavy burden. Physical signs like weight loss, muscle wasting, and frailty start to show, making it clear just how far-reaching alcohol's impact can be.

This journey takes a toll not only on our physical health but on our spirit. Memory fades, cognitive functions decline, and, in severe cases, alcohol-related dementia can develop. Infections, organ failure, and other complications are often the end result, a sobering reminder of how destructive alcohol can be over time. But it's important to remember that this progression isn't set in stone. Genetics, overall health, drinking patterns, and access to support all play a role, and with early intervention, the trajectory can change. There's hope in knowing that even small steps toward recovery can help us reclaim our health and our lives, allowing us to restore what alcohol once tried to take away.

Living with both alcoholism and co-occurring mental health conditions often takes a toll on one's sense of responsibility and conscientiousness. The challenges of mental health struggles layered on top of addiction can make daily life feel like a constant uphill battle, where staying grounded and focused feels out of reach. This cycle makes it harder to keep up with responsibilities, and it can leave many feeling discouraged in their recovery journey. There's a sense of always wanting more but feeling like it's never quite enough—a need that seems endless.

Navigating recovery can be especially tricky when it comes to non-alcoholic beers and mocktails. These alternatives can seem like a safe middle ground but often come with risks for those in early sobriety. Many treatment counselors and those who've walked the road of recovery for years recommend avoiding them altogether, especially at first. For some, they were never drawn to the taste of alcohol itself, so steering clear isn't difficult. For others, a well-crafted brew or a virgin cocktail can be tempting, and having these options around might feel like a comfort.

But it's important to remember that early sobriety is fragile, and even small triggers can lead us back down old paths. Alcohol-free options are becoming more common in bars and restaurants, but for someone working to protect their recovery, they may be best approached with caution—or avoided altogether. Every person's journey is different, and knowing one's triggers is essential. New sobriety is like a young plant; it needs the right environment to grow. That means changing up the people and places we surround ourselves with and avoiding old habits that could pull us back.

In the end, staying vigilant and surrounding ourselves with a supportive team is what helps keep us on track. Early recovery is a time of rebuilding—a chance to focus on creating new routines, new connections, and a new sense of self. With each step, we're learning to protect our sobriety, not just from the obvious threats but from the subtle ones that can sneak up on us if we're not careful.

CHAPTER FOUR

THE QUARTERBACK: A BALANCED ATTACK

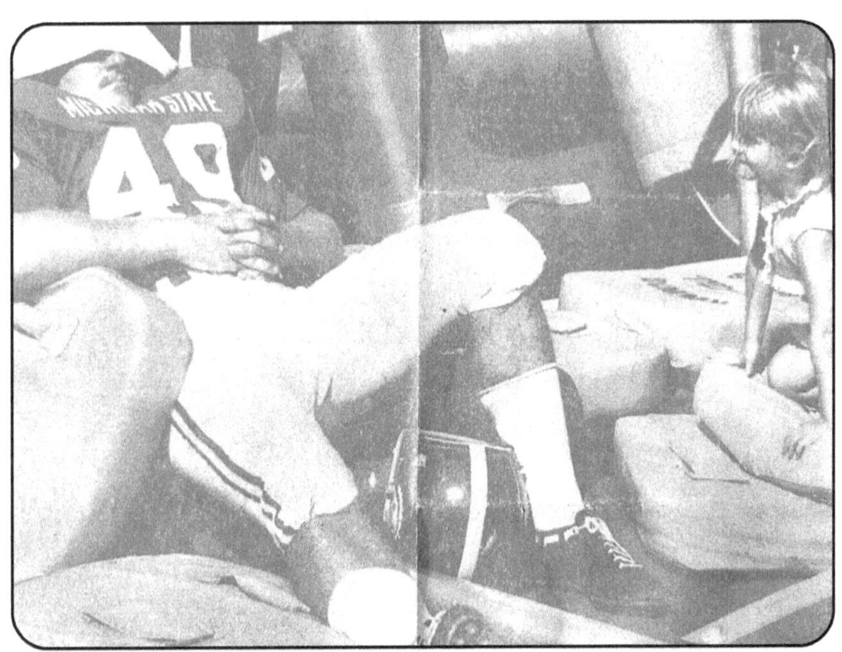

MAYA WASHINGTON, AN ACCOMPLISHED WRITER, PRODUCER, and scholar, has built an incredible career while honoring the legacy of her father, Gene Washington, former Minnesota Viking wide receiver. Maya's influence extends beyond her writing and production; she is also a passionate advocate for children's theater in Minneapolis, nurturing young talent and creating spaces where every child can find a voice.

Gene Washington, a fellow Spartan, was among a groundbreaking group of All-American players recruited by Michigan State's legendary coach, Duffy Daugherty. At that time, seeing Black athletes recruited to major programs was a rarity. Most teams in the major conferences had no more than a few Black players, if any at all. Duffy's leadership in the 1960s did more than build winning teams—it challenged the racial barriers in college football and laid the foundation for true integration. By the late '60s, nearly half the players on my own teams were Black athletes, talented men who brought grit, determination, and pride to the field.

This history resonates deeply with me, reminding me that being a Spartan has always meant standing for something larger than ourselves. It's about the pride we carry not just for winning titles, but for pushing past boundaries, making room for all who aspire to greatness, and paving the way for others. It's yet another reason why I am proud to be a Spartan.

Late in 2022, I took my young grandsons to a charming church in downtown Minneapolis to see Maya Washington's heartwarming production of The Velveteen Rabbit. This story has always held a special place in my family, cherished by both my daughters as they grew up. Watching my grandsons become captivated by this tale of love, authenticity, and transformation was a moment that felt beautifully familiar yet profoundly new.

In many ways, *The* Velveteen Rabbit reflects my own journey. Much like that little rabbit, I spent years feeling unworthy, unseen, as if I didn't quite belong in the world around me. But life has a way of shaping us, of polishing our rough edges through hardship and resilience. Over time, through mistakes, growth, and the grace of those around me, I began to understand what it meant to be "real." Just like the rabbit, I learned that becoming real isn't always easy or comfortable—it's a journey through vulnerability, transformation, and, ultimately, finding your true self.

As I watched my grandsons marvel at the story, I was filled with gratitude for this generational thread, for the ways stories like these can mirror our own lives and remind us that authenticity isn't something we're born with but something we earn along the way.

My battles with alcohol mirrored the Velveteen Rabbit's journey—searching for love, acceptance, and a place in the world. I, too, felt worn and tattered by life's challenges, struggling to find worth in a state where I felt hollow and distant from my true self. Recovery, like the love that transforms the rabbit, was a journey toward becoming real, not only in the eyes of others but to myself.

Through sobriety, I began to shed the worn parts of my life—the masks, the doubts, the need to numb myself. Piece by piece, I uncovered someone authentic beneath it all. I realized that becoming real wasn't about regaining perfection; it was about fully embracing my scars and the lessons they held. Through connection, vulnerability, and the community I found in recovery, I slowly discovered a self I hadn't known—one that was raw, but strong, flawed, but finally whole.

This path hasn't been easy, and I've come to see that, much like in *The Velveteen Rabbit*, becoming real is the gift of a lifetime. I now know a kind of happiness that no "buzz" could ever replace—a steady joy that grows deeper with each day of sobriety. In these moments of clarity and connection, I see that my story isn't just my own; it's one of hope, resilience, and the powerful healing that love and acceptance bring.

For those of us who have wrestled with addiction, the journey toward authenticity offers a sense of fulfillment far beyond any high we ever chased. It's a new kind of peace, and best of all, it's real.

Alcoholics often find themselves in a cycle of emotional instability, shaped by layers of neurochemical, psychological, and social factors that can feel overpowering:

1. **Neurochemical Shifts**: Alcohol deeply impacts brain chemistry, altering neurotransmitters like serotonin and dopamine, which are essential for mood regulation. Over time, these shifts contribute to mood imbalances that aren't just physical or psychological; they are part of the core struggle in fighting this disease.

2. **Coping Through Drinking**: For many, alcohol becomes the main method to manage pain and disappointment. At first, it might soothe the edges of a bad day, but as dependency grows, it becomes the only way to feel normal. This reliance traps us in a cycle, where the act of drinking is no longer for pleasure but simply to feel balanced—until even that fragile stability breaks.

3. **Withdrawal's Grip**: Without alcohol, withdrawal symptoms can hit hard, with waves of anxiety, irritability, and unpredictable mood swings. These symptoms create a barrier, both mental and physical, that makes each day without drinking an uphill battle.

4. **Life Pressures Intensified**: Alcoholism often brings with it a series of stressors—strained relationships, work struggles, financial instability, or legal issues. Instead of serving as an escape, alcohol magnifies these challenges, which in turn worsen emotional instability.

5. **Mental Health Challenges**: Depression, anxiety, and other mental health conditions frequently walk hand-in-hand with alcoholism. Each feeds into the other, amplifying emotional swings and making recovery feel like a more distant hope.

6. **Isolation's Weight**: The consequences of chronic alcohol use often lead to isolation. Friends grow distant, family relationships strain, and the circle closes in. This isolation leaves individuals with a heightened sense of loneliness and emotional distress, a feeling that many alcoholics know too well.

Together, these factors form a web of emotional instability, making recovery a deeply personal and challenging journey. But understanding these layers can be the first step. When we recognize the complexity of emotional pain behind alcoholism, we start to see why it's so vital to approach recovery with empathy, patience, and a willingness to untangle one layer at a time.

Alcoholics often find rebellion woven into their drinking behaviors, driven by complex motivations that extend far beyond the bottle itself:

1. **Defiance as a Form of Expression**: For many, drinking is a form of rebellion—a way to push back against societal norms, family pressures, or authority. This drive to defy can linger, even in sobriety, reminding us to remain aware of this rebellious streak and redirect it into healthier expressions of autonomy.

2. **Escaping the Grind**: Alcohol offers a taste of freedom from life's daily constraints, sometimes even from mundane routines. What begins as a momentary escape can lead to riskier behaviors,

as individuals let loose their frustrations and embrace rebellion in search of relief from a life that feels too controlled.

3. **Forging an Identity**: During adolescence or early adulthood, drinking often becomes an emblem of identity. For some, drinking recklessly serves as a badge of independence, a symbol of individuality—and in some cases, of defiance. Recklessness often takes center stage, allowing them to feel like they're crafting a "rebellious" persona, even as it pulls them deeper into dependency.

4. **Unspoken Emotions**: Rebellion sometimes becomes the only language to express deeper emotional turmoil. For those coping with buried pain, anger, or frustration, alcohol-fueled defiance is a form of communication—a raw way of signaling dissatisfaction with life's circumstances and escaping emotions that feel too heavy to bear.

5. **The Influence of Peers and Cultural Norms**: In social settings that glorify heavy drinking or rebellious behavior, individuals may feel a strong pull to conform. "Hazing" rituals and the pressures of belonging can create environments where heavy drinking feels like a rite of passage, entangling one's sense of self with the act of rebellion.

6. **Hiding Insecurities Behind Defiance**: For some, rebellious acts offer a temporary boost to self-image, a way to cover up feelings of inadequacy or low self-worth. The thrill of rebellion can feel like empowerment, masking deeper insecurities that surface as soon as the effects of alcohol wear off.

These rebellious tendencies are often a byproduct of seeking freedom, identity, or self-worth, albeit through damaging choices. Recognizing these drives for what they truly are—a search for meaning and acceptance—can be a profound step forward. By channeling that defiant spirit into positive, purposeful actions, we can begin to build a life that honors our independence without the need for self-sabotage.

A rebellious streak often weaves itself into the cycles of alcohol use, intensifying the struggle for sobriety. Each act of defiance, while seeming to offer freedom, often serves to reinforce dependency, making the path to recovery even steeper.

In countless group meetings over the years, I've found a shared understanding among us alcoholics—a mosaic of traits, struggles, and stories. Each personal account echoes a part of another's journey, which reveals the common personality traits so many of us carry. Our stories lay bare what we were like, what happened, and who we are today. And in this shared understanding, there's comfort and a sense of kinship that is no longer surprising but profoundly connecting.

This illness we face, alcoholism, is forged by both nature and nurture. Genetics can account for 40-60% of the risk of developing an alcohol use disorder, as studies tell us, capturing just how deeply embedded this illness can be in our biology. Yet, our environments, relationships, and life experiences shape our paths as well.

The chemistry behind it is complex: specific genes may influence how alcohol metabolizes in our bodies and how each of us responds to it, which can be a hidden trap, creating vulnerabilities without us even knowing it. The journey to sobriety often reveals how much of this disease stems from a place beyond immediate choice. But with understanding, we regain some power—knowledge becomes a cornerstone in building a life beyond these cycles.

Our journeys differ, but the path toward healing is universally strengthened by self-acceptance and connection. Recognizing these factors doesn't absolve us from responsibility; rather, it equips us to reclaim our lives, armed with awareness and resilience. Together, we find a way forward, knowing that shared experience is the bedrock of recovery.

Family history is one of the strongest threads that weave through the fabric of alcoholism, hinting at its psychological depth. Having a family member who struggles with alcoholism increases the risk of developing similar issues, suggesting a hereditary link. But the picture isn't simple. Families share more than just genetics; they share environments, norms, and daily habits that profoundly influence our earliest perceptions of alcohol.

For those who see alcoholism as primarily a product of nurture, family attitudes play a defining role. Growing up in an environment where drinking is normalized—or perhaps even encouraged—can shape one's outlook on alcohol in powerful, often lasting ways. The routines, behaviors, and unspoken rules we absorb as children echo through adulthood, often setting the stage for how we cope with life's challenges. And in some settings, like military families, the prevalence of alcohol use is strikingly higher, underscoring how environment can fuel risk.

This complexity deepens when considering cultural factors. Statistics reveal that certain nationalities, communities, and ethnic groups experience either heightened or surprisingly low rates of alcohol use. In some cultures, drinking is woven into social fabric and ritual, while others view it with caution or stigma. This duality reminds us that alcohol dependency isn't shaped by a single cause but by an intricate interplay of factors.

Alcoholism emerges from this blend of genetic predisposition and life experience, pushing many into a cycle that feels inevitable. Yet, while understanding these influences may not offer an easy fix, it empowers us to choose differently. Recognizing the roots of our struggle—and the way family, culture, and environment feed it—can shift our focus from blame to awareness, an essential step on the road to recovery.

For effective treatment, it's essential to recognize the complexity of alcoholism, blending medical, psychological, and social support to address the varied layers of this condition. The journey isn't straightforward; it demands attention to both the mind and the body, each with its distinct needs and challenges.

Alcoholic cravings differ greatly from those of non-alcoholics, and understanding this difference is crucial for recovery. These cravings don't just emerge from a desire to drink but often from a profound urgency—a mix of emotional emptiness and impulse that feels only soothed by reaching for alcohol. While a non-alcoholic may have occasional cravings without feeling compelled to act on them, for us, the cravings are frequent and intense, woven into the very fabric of our brain chemistry. They're triggered by cues in our environment, stress, social settings, and sometimes arise out of the blue, each one pulling at the resolve to stay sober.

Physically, cravings are tied to dependence. Over time, our brains adapt to alcohol's influence, changing how we process pleasure and regulate stress. These cravings are relentless and often accompanied by withdrawal symptoms like anxiety, irritability, and physical discomfort. Emotionally, the craving runs even deeper. Alcohol becomes a means to regulate pain, to mask trauma, depression, or even the small but persistent burdens of daily life. Our brains become wired to depend on it, and it can feel nearly impossible to resist, even with the knowledge of the damage done.

This difference—the compulsion, the frequency, the emotional need—is what makes the cravings of alcoholics distinct. Unlike the occasional desire that a non-alcoholic might feel, ours often become all-encompassing, urging us forward despite the consequences. And only by recognizing these differences can we hope to shape a treatment that provides both support and understanding.

Understanding the Transition from Desire to Craving

Addiction doesn't begin with the first drink; it begins with a simple desire. Over time, this desire deepens into something far more consuming. To understand this, we need to explore the factors that turn a simple "want" into an all-consuming "need."

1) Reinforcement: From Wanting to Needing

When we experience pleasure from obtaining something we desire, our brain's reward system reinforces this behavior. We're hardwired to seek that same pleasure again and again, intensifying our need. First, we want it; then we need it. The object of our desire becomes secondary—we simply crave the feeling. At first, we chase a buzz. Then, we keep going to feel normal. Finally, we're drinking just to get by, and anything less feels impossible.

2) Emotional Attachment: Cravings Born from Comfort and Escape

Emotional ties to certain desires make cravings all the stronger. Often, this attachment forms early on, when we link comfort, security, or an escape from pain to a specific food, substance, or habit. Many of us began drinking because it made us feel good; then, we drank to feel normal. Eventually, we drank because we had to. For alcoholics, cravings aren't merely a preference—they're deeply rooted in the desire to cope with discomfort or avoid negative emotions.

3) Habituation: The Familiar Traps Us

Habits are powerful, and repetition reinforces them. Consider the routine of stopping at the same bar after work, settling into the same chair, seeing the same faces. For those of us who've struggled with addiction, this cycle of comfort becomes an unbreakable trap. It's like the bar from *Cheers*—a place where everyone knows your name and you're caught in the comforting web of familiarity. Soon, one drink isn't enough, and we stay longer, drink more, and become addicted to the illusion of "more." The familiar leads us back time and again, each visit stretching longer and feeling harder to end.

4)   The Lack of Self-Regulation: Why Half-Measures Fail

Without solid impulse control, we quickly lose the ability to moderate desires. Temporary fixes, like changing the people we drink with or the places we go, only patch the surface. We convince ourselves that switching from hard liquor to beer, or only drinking at home, will solve the problem. But it's a false solution. In meetings, we often hear the well-worn phrase: "Half-measures availed us nothing." True healing requires a deeper approach—a complete, honest removal and replacement of our "patches," no matter how uncomfortable it feels.

Exploring Addiction's Hold on Us

Addiction runs deeper than a behavior. Our desires and cravings are complex, fed by emotional needs, past attachments, and habits. Recognizing these roots helps us understand why the cycle continues and reminds us that recovery requires honesty, resilience, and a commitment to rebuilding our lives without those temporary fixes. Sobriety isn't just about saying no—it's about breaking free from the powerful traps that kept us from finding true peace.

The shared stories from others in recovery offer more than just comfort; they're windows into experiences that, while different from our own, echo many of the same struggles. Yet, these stories are not here for comparison. When we start measuring our own patterns against others, sneaky justifications creep in: "She's been married four times, I've only been married twice," or "I only lost one job, and he lost three." It becomes easy to downplay our challenges by measuring them against others' misfortunes, telling ourselves, "At least my liver still works," or "I'm not nearly as out of control as he is." In recovery, what's essential is to connect with others, to relate—not to compare. Every individual journey to sobriety is valid on its own terms.

In this journey, you may find a "Group of Drunks" (GOD) who support you in ways you never expected. This group may even become the foundation of a higher power in your life, a source of strength and resilience you never thought possible. Some people find this support through Christian faith, expressing their gratitude to God as if He helped them score a personal victory. But if this doesn't resonate with you, that's okay. Sobriety doesn't require any particular belief system; it only requires the courage to find support in what feels right to you.

Whether or not faith is central to your journey, there's no denying that the concept of a higher power is woven throughout recovery literature. The AA Big Book, for instance, touches frequently on God. If every mention of God were removed, the pages left would barely fill a thin booklet. It's described as "spiritual, not religious," yet faith is undeniably a part of it. For those who draw strength from spirituality, this can be grounding. But for others, the value lies in simply connecting to a sense of guidance, regardless of the form it takes.

The real strength of recovery lies not in dogma but in the journey itself. It's a deeply personal path that each person shapes according to their needs, rooted in support, compassion, and acceptance. Sobriety is not about comparing stories, beliefs, or struggles. It's about finding what drives you toward a better life, discovering what strengthens you, and celebrating that growth on your terms. Embrace the stories of others for the camaraderie they offer, but remember: your journey is uniquely yours, shaped by your own experiences and needs.

Cravings, often misunderstood as purely physical symptoms of addiction, are often deeply rooted in the psychological landscape of our lives. For many, they echo unmet emotional needs, unresolved anxieties, or lingering scars from traumatic experiences. Each individual's cravings are as unique as their life story, shaped by the nuances of personality and past.

Growing up, I carried a sadness I couldn't fully understand. It was simply a constant companion, woven into my day-to-day life.

My parents were young, still figuring out their own lives and not particularly warm or demonstrative. I don't hold it against them now—they did what they could, I suppose. Much of my time was spent with my mother's family, helping out in their country general store. I learned so many skills there at a young age—lessons in responsibility and independence, yes, but with very little of the affection or encouragement a young kid longs for.

I rarely saw my paternal grandparents even though they lived nearby. My happiest childhood memories come from time spent with my mother's younger sister, Aunt Joyce, and her husband, Uncle John. They seemed genuinely happy and gave me glimpses of a warmer side of family life. They even took me along on their "dates" before they were married, treating me like I was part of their world in a way that felt special. It was a comfort I didn't get at home.

Later, I understood that my mother held a lot of jealousy toward her younger sister. I'd heard her describe herself bitterly as the "workhorse" while Aunt Joyce was the "show horse," seemingly favored by their parents. The echoes of this dynamic became part of my own inner world. As kids, we absorb so much from our environments. Those early experiences set the stage, and while family members may act out of their own hurts and unmet needs, it leaves lasting imprints on us.

It took me years to understand how these underlying, formative moments played into my own behaviors and cravings. So many of us reach for something—alcohol, drugs, validation—to fill the spaces left by early emotional gaps. Understanding where these cravings come from, acknowledging the role of our unique histories, helps illuminate a path toward healing. For me, it's meant learning not just about recovery, but about self-compassion, resilience, and the ability to rewrite those old stories in a way that strengthens my journey toward sobriety.

The mantra was clear in our household: hard work was everything, and if you worked hard, rewards would naturally follow. My family lived by this idea, almost as if it were a law of physics, as if dedication and perseverance alone could order the universe. My grandparents, especially Grandpa Anderson, embodied this mindset. The government's only role, in his eyes, was to build roads and extinguish fires. Everything else—compassion, generosity—was the duty of churches, missionaries, and local communities. We were a model of right-wing conservatism, strict in our beliefs and our definitions of success. My grandfather may well have been the most steadfast, uncompromising conservative I've ever known.

But beneath the lessons of self-reliance and relentless pursuit, I began to internalize an unintended message. In striving for everything I wanted, I was somehow missing everything I needed. Soothing myself through success and hard work became second nature. I didn't question it, but in the end, I was left without the kind of love and emotional nourishment that no reward or achievement could provide. It took me years to understand how much I'd sacrificed at the altar of this belief in self-sufficiency, mistaking it for love or validation. It was an unhealthy pattern that took root early on, a survival mechanism that left its mark on my journey in ways I'm still unraveling.

For much of my early life, I was an observer, watching the ways my parents handled their roles within the family. My father, slipping further into his alcoholism, grew increasingly distant, while my mother's codependent tendencies took root, creating a household that functioned in shadows. I saw the impact on my younger siblings— how they were subjected to an emotional coldness that became normal in our home. Their treatment mirrored my own, though I didn't realize until much later just how deeply these dynamics affected me. For years, these experiences sat beyond my awareness, shaping me quietly from the background, influencing my decisions and understanding of myself.

In the absence of healthy affection and support, I developed ways to manage my unmet emotional needs, ways that, while effective in the short term, were unhealthy in the long run. Discipline at home was not the supportive, guiding hand it should have been, but instead a random, inconsistent system of punishment. By the time I was ten, I was already forming plans to leave, figuring out how to build a life beyond these walls. Being in this environment, with its lack of affection and chaotic structure, fueled my desires and my need for something more. It wasn't long before I discovered that temporary satisfactions could stand in for deeper validation. This external validation became a close ally, helping me feel "okay" in a life that often felt confusing and emotionally barren.

Most of my childhood was spent seeking solace in solitude. I longed to be alone, retreating from the volatile environment around me, finding comfort in my own space. Over time, this need for solitude only grew, becoming a part of me I never outgrew. It was a shield and a refuge, allowing me to navigate the complexities of unmet needs and unspoken pain—layers of my story that I am only now beginning to truly unpack and understand.

Growing up, my friendships were few but meaningful, mostly revolving around my teammates and the kids in my neighborhood. They were the closest I had to a social circle, but even then, I often felt like an outsider. As I got older, my focus shifted to girls—attracted by their intelligence, their complexity, and something deeper I couldn't quite name. That interest began early, shaping much of how I navigated my teenage years.

Despite my growing curiosity, I was most at ease alone in nature, exploring the woods and creek banks surrounding our family farm. Those places became my personal escape, a world away from the pressures and expectations at home. I spent countless hours there, building makeshift huts, forts, and campsites, almost as if I were mapping out a path to freedom. These secluded hideouts provided a sense of control and comfort, and with each fort I built or animal I hunted, I felt a step closer to the independence I craved. Looking back, I realize I was subconsciously preparing for my eventual escape, seeking solace in these quiet corners of the world that seemed so far removed from my family life.

"Never be afraid to sit in silence, it's your greatest asset." (Robin Sharma)

CHAPTER FIVE

THE OFFENSIVE LINE—GAP PROTECTION

THE FIRST TIME I DRANK ENOUGH TO FEEL THAT BUZZ, I WAS still in high school. I hadn't expected alcohol to click with me as strongly as it did. The sensation was something I immediately liked. But back then, I knew better than to risk drinking too often—the penalties for getting caught were steep, especially for someone like me, a three-sport athlete with no off-season. For a while, I managed to keep drinking to a minimum, mindful of everything I had to lose.

By then, my identity was firmly anchored in my athletic success. I wasn't only an athlete but a good student, pushed by my parents to excel in everything. There was no leniency, no sliding by on anything less than top performance. Grades weren't given away easily then, and teachers weren't pressured to inflate them to appease demanding parents. My parents' high expectations had driven me to work hard, and it paid off. I graduated in the top ten of my class, even serving as President of the National Honor Society. It felt like proof of what a little extra effort could accomplish—an accomplishment I could hold onto, even when everything else felt uncertain.

My maternal grandfather had thought it was charming to let me sip his beer when I was barely more than a toddler. I don't know if this early introduction to alcohol had any impact on my eventual struggles, but it sent subtle signals about its importance. I grew up seeing beer as something integral to special moments, even those spent fishing with him. Every Wednesday—his only day off—he'd load up a cooler with beer, soda, pickled ring bologna, saltines, and a brick of sharp cheese. We'd spend the day on his boat, fishing quietly under the open sky. Summers were marked by these Wednesdays together, and I was lucky. Those times were simple and happy.

There's a whole spectrum of "drunk stories" out there. Some are lighthearted and amusing; others, tragic and unsparing. No one gets to choose how their story unfolds. I think back on those fishing trips fondly, even as I wonder how much they planted the idea that alcohol was a natural part of a good time.

One memory from college stands out. During a summer break, my wife and I were staying at my parents' cottage at Eight Point Lake in Northern Michigan. I was training at Central Michigan University, and we'd invited my grandparents up for a day on the lake. It was early morning, and Wendy and I were still in bed when I heard my grandfather's unmistakable laugh echo across the lake. He was already settled in, cooler at his side, probably anticipating the calm that fishing brings and that small, familiar comfort of beer at his elbow.

These were my roots, laid out clearly. The closeness of family, the habit of turning to alcohol to mark the simple joys.

When I opened the door, there they were—my grandparents, standing with their familiar smiles. As we moved into the kitchen, my grandpa's first words after "hello" were, "Are you ready for a beer?" I laughed and said, "Grandpa, I haven't even had my coffee yet." It was always clear to him that any good moment could be made better with a cold beer. It took me years to learn that wasn't always the case.

My grandpa's connection to alcohol and social spaces had deep roots. Back in the 1930s, before he bought a general store in Woodbury, Michigan, he ran a barbershop on the main street of Lansing, near the state capital. Those old shops weren't just about haircuts; they were community spaces, especially for men. His shop had barber chairs in the front, pool tables in the middle, and, at the back, a few card tables near the cigar counter. A steady stream of cigar smoke and the occasional hidden bottle gave the place a gritty, comforting ambiance. Customers would spend hours there, and some never got around to the haircut.

Just before World War II, my grandparents bought a small general store on M-66, the main two-lane road running north through Michigan. This store was a whole world unto itself, packed with everything from groceries to hardware, and even a lunch counter where my grandma served coffee and sandwiches. On the north side of the store, he set up a little barber area in front of a walk-in cooler, just around the corner from the meat counter, where he'd cut hair between chatting with customers.

To a kid like me, this was paradise. It was a place of community, connection, and in my grandfather's eyes, a good place for a drink. But looking back, it's clear that my relationship with alcohol was shaped by these early memories. I absorbed the message that alcohol and camaraderie went hand in hand, that any outing—a day of fishing, a stop by the barbershop—could be enhanced by a drink. As I grew older, I realized how hard it was to untangle myself from these associations. Those early lessons around family, fun, and alcohol stayed with me long after I left my grandparents' store behind.

By the front door sat the cash register, with rows of liquor bottles stacked behind the counter, their colors and labels almost like a beacon to those walking in. This was where I spent so much of my young life, a world that ran on long days and steady work, where each task had its place and purpose. Outside, we pumped gas and checked oil for customers, who often stopped to buy a few things and chat with my grandparents. My grandfather was proud of the large wooden wheels of cheese aging above the shelves, known for their sharp, rich flavor after years of careful tending. The store had almost everything you could need, including the tools and bait for rabbit hunting and fishing supplies stored out back in the old horse stable, alongside my grandmother's gardening tools for her magnificent iris beds.

A sweet cherry tree stood tall in my grandmother's garden, producing a bounty of cherries every summer without fail. That tree, with its unchanging yield year after year, mirrored the constancy of life around the store, where the rhythm of chores and interactions set a dependable pace.

By the time I was nine or ten, I was stocking shelves, pumping gas, grinding beef and pork for sausage, and counting back change with the old-fashioned precision my grandfather insisted on. "You're not paying attention to your money unless it's face-up and all pointing in the same direction," he would remind me countless times. Hard work and responsibility weren't just expected; they were drilled into me. There was no excuse to slack off, no reason to do things halfway. Generosity and compassion? That was for the church to teach. Here, we worked and provided, and I learned early that hard work had its own reward.

This was my world during those formative years, and I came to understand the deep satisfaction that comes from putting in the effort, from knowing you've earned what you have. It was a life centered around duty, routine, and resilience, and while my grandparents were generous with my pay, the real lesson was about work: that it was always worth doing, and that it always, in some way, paid off.

Good memories and bad memories alike drive our habits. Over the years, I've had many friends who were heavy drinkers—some who went on to become alcoholics, and others who didn't. Sometimes, the choice isn't ours to make. It took me time to accept this, and even longer to realize that I didn't have to carry shame or resentment about it. I've come to a place of peace with it now, and I know that for some of us, like Yogi Bear would say, we're maybe even a little "smarter than the average bear" because of the journey.

Recognizing that I had crossed the line into addiction didn't happen overnight. It took fifteen years. Looking back, that gradual slide from casual to controlled to consumed was almost imperceptible. A lot of Bill W's early followers shared a similar path. Many started drinking around twenty, and by their mid-thirties, the line had been crossed. In those days, AA was a circle of people with similar lives—steady jobs, families, professional commitments—yet here we all were, brought together by a struggle that connected us more deeply than any of those things. It didn't matter where we'd come from or what we did for a living. In those rooms, we became a team, with sobriety as our common goal.

The pull of alcohol is powerful, no matter who you are. In many ways, addiction is like a game—a tough, relentless one where the score keeps changing. And to succeed, we have to understand both the rules and our own tendencies. We learn to recognize when a desire tips into craving, and when that craving becomes a threat. But it's not a journey we walk alone. Just as in sports, there's a team behind each of us. For some, it's the familiar circle at AA; for others, it's family, friends, or even just the voices that ground us, reminding us why we started. In recovery, we're coached by the people we trust, encouraged by the friends who've walked this road with us, and strengthened by the knowledge that we don't have to do it alone.

In those early meetings, surrounded by others who understood the fight, we found a sense of community—a relief in knowing we didn't have to tackle this beast on our own. And maybe that's one of the biggest lessons I've learned: recovery isn't a solo sport. It's a team effort, and when we play together, we're a hell of a lot stronger.

In the early days, addiction often took fifteen years or so to fully take hold—fifteen years to move from that first drink to a place of undeniable dependency. But that timeline feels like a relic of another era. Today, we're seeing it happen faster, with earlier starts and stronger substances pulling people down more quickly. It's a heartbreak to watch; even teenagers are battling full-blown addiction by the time they're eighteen or nineteen. Some never make it to adulthood without finding themselves at rock bottom.

This shift has redefined what it means to be an addict and even changed how we talk about "functioning alcoholics"—those who can hold onto their jobs or relationships just enough to keep the illusion of control. I have friends and family who drink heavily, and I often wonder if they're just skirting the edge or if they, too, will eventually stumble. I don't know how they manage it or what keeps them just out of the addiction spiral. But I do know that, for me, the idea of going back—of having a magical chance to be a "normal" drinker—no longer holds any appeal. And for many in AA, this kind of confidence is something to be wary of; they remind us that sobriety is fragile, a balance to be respected rather than taken for granted.

One debate that's come up time and again in recovery circles is "recovery" versus "recovered." It's a loaded discussion, a tug-of-war between the idea of an ongoing journey and the hope for a settled peace. No matter the side you take, it's all about patience and persistence. Addiction teaches you that much. And whether you see yourself as always in recovery or someday reaching a place of "recovered," there's power in knowing that every step counts, every bit of progress is real.

In this game, sobriety isn't just a solo mission—it's a team sport. Recovery is about the people who back you up, the coaches who remind you why you started, the teammates who understand the struggle. Together, we learn that every choice, every practice, makes a difference. And when we embrace that spirit, we're playing not just to survive but to win.

Confidence in sobriety can be a fine line to walk—one moment you're feeling solid, and the next, a single slip can unravel it all. It's a delicate balance, and some folks in AA have made it clear that overconfidence is a dangerous sign. I get it. For anyone in recovery, cockiness is a red flag waving bright as day.

Thinking back, I realize I was no stranger to the edges of overconfidence myself. My college years were filled with football at Michigan State University, which was as much about intense hits on the field as it was about drinking and experimenting with new highs. That was the era—hard-hitting football, and for me, a thrill in every solid tackle. My brief NFL career as a linebacker took me through camps with two Super Bowl teams, the '72 Dolphins and '73 Vikings. I never got beyond training camps and exhibition games, though; my time was short, and eventually, I traded my spot for a coaching job back in Michigan.

Back then, NFL players weren't household names, and most of us worked outside jobs in the offseason just to make ends meet. Minimum salaries were a fraction of what they are today—$13,200 a year. My signing bonus was less than what my dental insurance just paid out for a root canal repair. Still, it was a taste of a different life, a flash of a dream that many of us chased. The competitive rush, the camaraderie—it's an intensity I still find echoes of today, even on the golf course when a solid hit still feels like a win.

That craving for the next hit, the next thrill—it doesn't disappear when you leave the game. In recovery, it shows up in different ways, the challenge now to find healthy ways to keep that edge without falling back into old patterns. For some of us, recovery is a lifelong sport. I don't think I'll ever "finish" it, and I'm okay with that. Every day is practice, every year a new season. We don't get a final whistle; we just keep playing the game, working toward something better, and staying grateful for the teammates and coaches who help us stay on course.

Sobriety, for me, is a full-contact sport in its own way. It's about taking the hits and still getting back up, relying on the team around you, and finding new ways to push forward. I may not be in a stadium anymore, but I'm still in the game, and every step forward feels like the kind of win that matters most.

Looking back, it's no surprise that my experience would eventually be mirrored in Pete Gent's North Dallas Forty. Football culture in those days was a fast track to "off the hook" behavior. Bigger bodies needed bigger pills, and the unofficial motto became, "the bigger they are, the bigger the pill." For someone like me, whose addiction was already brewing, it was the perfect storm. I didn't just go along with it—I embraced it.

Speed, anabolic steroids, sedatives… they were all part of the game. For us, it wasn't even controversial. In those years, team doctors handed out pills like they were handing out game day snacks. "Dianabol" became a nickname for me by my last two years at Michigan State, a nod to the steroids that were becoming a daily ritual. My life at that point revolved around extreme powerlifting and building myself up in ways that were as unsustainable as they were addictive. I even trained alongside Roger Callard, a younger guy with big dreams who would go on to win Mr. Universe and make his mark in television and film.

Football demanded intensity, a commitment to winning that sometimes blurred the lines between dedication and obsession. For me, addiction was right there in the mix. I realize now that I was feeding something deeper, a need for control, or maybe it was just the thrill of it all. The rush I felt after a hard hit on the field carried over into every other aspect of my life, especially when it came to substances.

But just as football taught me to take a hit, recovery has taught me to understand why I sought those hits in the first place. Addiction is a lot like the game; you're part of a team, and no matter how strong you are, you're never strong enough alone. I came into sobriety with an ego, thinking I could handle it all solo. I was wrong. The real strength has come in leaning on others, in recognizing that addiction is not a battle to be fought single-handedly. The team of people who back me up, the new habits I've built to replace the old ones—these are the moves I rely on now.

If there's one thing I've learned, it's that sobriety is about embracing the highs and lows with humility, knowing that every day you show up is a win. The lessons from my football days still resonate, but they mean something different now. Today, it's not about winning the game for myself—it's about staying on the field for those who are playing beside me, learning to take the hits and still get back up. Sobriety, like football, is a team sport, and I'm proud to be part of it.

Addiction followed me into my working years, and the consequences came fast. I found myself in a role that many might consider respectable—a teacher and a coach. On paper, I was shaping young minds, pushing players to reach their potential, showing them how to dig deep. But as for being a role model? I wasn't anyone's picture of that. In fact, I stood out like a warning sign in the school district.

The superintendent made sure that new, young coaches and teachers knew to steer clear of me after hours. I was labeled a "bad influence," a lone wolf who took "my way or the highway" a bit too literally. I never quite fit the mold of the school environment, with my approach rubbing against the grain of what was considered appropriate or safe. And that need to be right at all costs didn't do me any favors—it ended up earning me official reprimands tucked neatly away in my personnel file.

I had a fire, a competitiveness that didn't switch off once I walked off the field. I wanted to win in every conversation, every decision. But that same drive, while powerful on game day, was misplaced in real life. It became a shadow side that others could see even when I couldn't. Addiction had started to shape how I approached everything, blinding me to the impact I was having on those around me.

In sobriety, I've come to understand that winning isn't about being right or getting your way every time. It's about connection, empathy, and knowing when to listen instead of push. Recovery has given me the chance to see these "reprimands" for what they really were—a sign that I had some personal growing to do. And, just like any team sport, this growth isn't a solo endeavor. It takes others, people who help us reflect on who we are and where we're headed, to show us that sometimes the best victories are the ones where we're willing to change, even when it's uncomfortable.

Being part of the recovery team means leaving ego at the door and embracing a new kind of strength—one that doesn't demand dominance but instead values humility. Every day, I'm learning to be a better teammate, a more honest role model. And if I'd known back then what I know now, I might have seen those warnings as an invitation to turn things around sooner. But today, I'm grateful to have the chance to keep working on it, both for myself and for the people I'm showing up for now.

During those years, I became a poor husband and father. My addiction pulled me farther and farther away from the people I loved most. I was rarely home when my wife or my daughters needed me. And even when I was, I wasn't truly present. There was always a tall tumbler within reach, a Manhattan in hand, the glass as much a fixture of my presence as my own face. This spiral lasted for years, creating a distance between us that I didn't fully grasp until long after sobriety began.

Recovery, as I've learned, isn't just about putting down the drink—it's about picking up the pieces. In facing my addiction, I had to look directly at what I'd done to my family. The pain, the neglect, the trust I'd shattered. This wasn't the work of a quick apology; it was an excavation, a commitment to address each scar I'd left. And that process doesn't end the moment you get sober. True healing requires honesty, patience, and a willingness to bear the weight of your actions. Making amends is the real work, and it demands that we face our past squarely, with no evasions. Only then can we begin to forgive ourselves, to move into the present with a sense of integrity.

Sobriety, I realized, doesn't automatically fix fractured relationships. My sobriety was only one piece of the puzzle. Repairing the deep-seated wounds I'd left behind meant earning back trust bit by bit, facing resentment that lingered like an unwelcome guest. Sobriety and "not drinking" aren't the same thing. The road back to my family's trust wasn't a sprint; it was a marathon, requiring time, grit, and what I can only describe as "working your ass off."

These days, I'm grateful for every step forward we've taken together. Recovery isn't just about finding freedom from addiction; it's about embracing the responsibility that comes with it. And for those of us in long-term recovery, it's a commitment we make not just to ourselves but to everyone we've impacted along the way.

My wake-up call came with a drunk driving charge, a 30-day stay at an inpatient treatment facility, and my first introduction to Alcoholics Anonymous. I can't say I walked in with the humility or gratitude the experience deserved, but a seed was planted. They say in treatment that if an alcoholic can take in just the first three steps, there's a chance. I held onto that idea, unsure of what would come next but realizing I couldn't keep going down the same path.

During those early days, I met a woman who would become one of the quiet yet profound memories of my recovery. Her name was Mary. She was tiny, elderly, and frail, brought in by ambulance, lying on a stretcher in a hospital gown as though any movement might break her. Mary looked as though she was clinging to life by a thread. But each day, we found ourselves sitting together in the hospital van, headed to our daily meetings at the Alano Club. Her transformation over the next thirty days was something I never could have imagined. She became stronger, more present, her once-empty eyes gaining a glimmer of hope.

Mary's journey reminded me that change, real change, could happen—even when we're starting from rock bottom. For me, she was proof that there was something worth striving for, that recovery could be more than a struggle. The work, the humility it required, wasn't about instant redemption. It was about discovering what hope looked like in its quiet, resilient way. I didn't know it then, but those thirty days would lay the foundation for everything I would come to understand about sobriety:

that it's a journey with teammates, each of us pushing forward, leaning on one another, and showing up even when we feel weak.

Looking back, I see now that Mary and I both needed each other, even if it was just to hold onto a fragile idea of hope. Her transformation gave me a glimpse of what was possible, even if my own path felt uncertain. That experience taught me that sometimes the smallest seeds can grow into the biggest changes. In recovery, it's those seeds, those moments of connection, that carry us forward, day by day.

Mary practically danced out of the hospital. She was transformed—a petite, well-dressed woman with bright eyes, a lightness in her step, and a renewed energy that was hard to believe. Seeing the toll that years of alcohol had taken on her was a sobering sight in itself. And even with this clear evidence in front of me, I struggled to fully connect it to my own journey. I was too stubborn, too unwilling to surrender, and far from ready to admit I needed to make a change.

In the years that followed, I've lost friends and family to this disease. I was lucky, incredibly lucky, that my own choices hadn't harmed or killed anyone else. Ultimately, I learned that an alcoholic's path has three inevitable options: jail, death, or sobriety. And with that realization, the early seeds planted in 1984—my first exposure to the first three steps of Alcoholics Anonymous—began to take root.

In the beginning, those steps felt like a lifeline, but it took time for me to truly understand their depth. AA was giving me a roadmap to a different way of living, but I had to learn to let go of my defenses and accept help. That journey wasn't quick or easy, but it marked the start of a lifelong commitment to a new path. It was a lesson in humility, acceptance, and learning to value the people who walked this journey with me—like Mary, who reminded me that even the heaviest burdens can be lifted when we find the strength to take that first step.

Looking back now, I can see how that time set me on course. It wasn't just about getting sober; it was about finding a purpose, a way to stay in the game even when things felt impossible. That journey has been my greatest challenge and, in many ways, my greatest gift.

I was ready to admit I was powerless, but surrender—that was an entirely different word, one that didn't exist in my vocabulary. To me, surrender meant weakness, and I wasn't about to give up that easily. So, there I was, begrudgingly attending AA meetings every week, moving through the motions but with little intention of truly letting go. I became a "dry drunk," white-knuckling my way through daily life, resisting every step. Sitting in the Greek Cathedral basement on Monday nights, I'd look around at the old-timers, laughing and chatting like they'd won the lottery, and I just didn't get it. Half measures, they'd say, "availed us nothing." I was halfway in, but I was still holding on.

Somewhere along this half-sober path, I rediscovered blackjack. With a degree in mathematics, I figured the odds were in my favor. Counting cards was easy, and I thought I could outsmart the casinos, beat the game, stay in control. Winning wasn't the issue. Keeping those winnings, however, was a different story. Walking away when I was up a couple of thousand was as tough as stopping after just one drink. Sometimes I managed it, sometimes I didn't. But one thing was clear— addiction had its grip on me, and I wasn't the one calling the shots.

At the same time, I was day trading commodities from my personal account, another gamble in a suit and tie. Every winning streak brought a rush, every loss stoked a need to recover it. I'd convinced myself I was in control, that I had the edge, but I was just feeding the same addiction in a different form. Kenny Rogers sang about knowing when to hold 'em and when to fold 'em, but to an addict, that line's meaningless. We're wired to keep going, long past the point of reason. The illusion of control was just another one of my half measures, one more way to keep from surrendering.

It took me a long time to realize that surrender doesn't mean weakness; it's the starting line. I was out there playing every game, gambling with my life, but refusing to acknowledge I was already losing. It wasn't until I stopped seeing surrender as defeat and started seeing it as a chance to get back in the game—for real—that I began to understand what those old-timers in the basement had been laughing about all along.

How could I even consider surrender? The Spartan motto practically ran through my veins: "Come Back With Your Shield Or On It." Surrender was for the weak, and weakness wasn't something I could afford. My upbringing reinforced this message—strength above all, never giving in. My father's silent expectations were clear. He had little respect for his own father, my Grandpa Barnum, who was a quiet man, a small dairy farmer with no interest in drink or conflict. He went to the United Brethren Church every Sunday, didn't touch a drop of alcohol, and from what I was told, he was seen as a pacifist, almost meek, by the men in town. They called him Buddy. And to my father, that name carried a certain sting. I could see that he saw Grandpa's gentleness as a flaw, a weakness. Ironically, my own father-in-law, from a nearby town, was known as Bud his whole life. But he was different—a second-generation hardware store owner, well-liked and respected, a man with a handshake you could trust.

Growing up with these men around me, I thought strength meant pushing forward, never bending, and certainly never stepping back. My brother-in-law now owns a successful beach restaurant and bowling alley, fittingly named "Buddy's On The Beach" after his father. Even surrounded by strong personalities, I couldn't help but think about Grandpa Barnum, spending his days behind a team of horses, tending to the dairy cows that demanded his care twice every single day. He'd work his fields for hours, uncovering arrowheads and relics left by the land's first inhabitants, slowly building a rock pile around Grandma's clothesline pole. It was like he was building a quiet legacy, one rock at a time.

The funny thing is, I was terrified of the giant rooster that roamed their yard. That bird seemed to embody every ounce of grit and persistence I struggled with, and it chased me any chance it got, always ready to put me in my place.

In sobriety, I've learned that strength isn't just the loudest voice in the room or the hardest hit. True strength is facing who you are and where you've come from, embracing the quiet legacies of people like Grandpa Barnum, who may have seemed unassuming but whose lives held a different kind of courage. Surrendering to sobriety didn't mean losing my strength; it meant reimagining what strength really is. It's humility, it's resilience, and sometimes it's even the quiet patience of a man who worked the land every day, finding peace in simple, steady work.

It took me years to understand that surrender isn't about giving up. It's about finding the wisdom to know when to let go, when to listen, and when to trust that there's more strength in humility than in the fiercest display of bravado.

Every Sunday morning before church, my grandmother would go out into the yard, catch a chicken, and take it to the clothesline, where she'd hang it up until she returned home to prepare Sunday dinner. She was practical and unflinching in her way, her compassion reserved for family rather than the demands of the farm. My father, though, didn't seem to understand this natural compassion that seemed to come so freely to the rest of his family. Perhaps he felt a kind of isolation, the same kind I'd come to feel as I grew up. I'll never know.

The Barnums weren't people of means, and life was lean. My dad often told the story of how he'd stop by the granary with an old gunny sack, grabbing a few oats or some wheat to sell on his way to pick up my mother. They'd laugh about it in later years, but as a kid, that was his ticket for a date night, and it showed me the subtle pride he carried, making ends meet on his own terms.

I spent little time with my paternal grandparents or my father's side of the family. My older cousins, aunts, and uncles were distant figures, familiar but seldom seen. One exception was an uncle with whom Dad and I would go "Up North" for deer hunting season. Northern Michigan, with its thick woods and abundance of deer, became a place where my father and I found a quiet understanding, even if words were few.

Those trips to the woods and my grandparents' farm were part of a legacy I didn't fully grasp at the time. My grandfather spent his days behind a team of horses, tending to his fields and milking the dairy cows morning and night. The farm was his world, and while plowing his fields, he'd come across arrowheads and other remnants left by Native Americans long before us. Each artifact ended up in a rock pile near Grandma's clothesline, a quiet collection of history accumulating around their home. It was a subtle reminder that life is layered, a mix of what came before and what we bring into it.

Sobriety has made me reflect on those memories differently, especially how the simplicity of their lives contrasted with the chaos I created in mine. My grandfather didn't leave a fortune, but he left behind a certain resilience, a legacy built by steady hands, quiet values, and an unspoken strength. His strength was different from what I once believed defined a man—it was patient, humble, rooted. And though it took me years to recognize it, that legacy has become part of my own journey toward recovery, showing me that true strength is found in understanding, humility, and the willingness to face life as it comes.

Opening day of deer season was practically a holiday for us. November 15th was sacred in rural Michigan, with schools clearing their schedules, boys off for a day or two to head out to the woods. It was such a big deal that, in 1965, I even turned down a chance to attend the "Game of the Century" between Michigan State and Notre Dame. That invitation was special—I'd been invited as a recruit by MSU's football coaches—but I already knew MSU was where I'd be committing. I chose hunting over the game, and years later, hundreds of thousands would claim they were there to witness it, even though I knew I'd been lucky enough to have had a seat waiting for me.

My relationship with my father was more complicated than any of those decisions. I sensed his embarrassment toward his family, though I was too young to fully understand it. He put distance between us and his past, and in some ways, that distance extended to me. As I grew up, he seemed to be focused on "keeping up with the Joneses" more than anything else, a habit that seeped into my own life in ways I'd later struggle to shake. In time, his discomfort with his family became something I mirrored—maybe even resented—as if he were embarrassed by where he came from. When my parents sold the small forty-acre farm I grew up on, it was another step away from that legacy, as if they were trading it in for something they hoped would feel like success.

After the move, I found myself driving back and forth to my old high school each day, unwilling to let go of my roots even as my parents tried to plant new ones. My dad's career in sales put him in the thick of the era of entertainment expense accounts and three-martini lunches. We moved into a shiny new house in a country club subdivision, right along the golf course. My parents wanted to fit into that world, but the truth was, they never quite did, and neither did I. That place felt foreign to me, like a costume that didn't fit, and I wasn't interested in playing the part. I was out.

Those moves and shifts shaped me more than I knew at the time. They taught me about authenticity, about how easily we can lose ourselves when we chase external validation. My father's attempts to distance himself from his past while reaching for something he thought mattered only created a void that would take me years to understand and even longer to confront. Sobriety has given me a chance to reexamine those years with a clearer perspective, to see how family history and identity weave into our lives, shaping our struggles and choices, even when we think we've left them behind.

In recovery, I've come to see that strength isn't about where you live or how you look to others; it's about facing who you are, where you come from, and what truly matters. Those early days of hunting, of grounding myself in something real, have become reminders that it's the simple, honest connections that truly last.

A few years later, I got my own taste of the "sociable salesman" life. Wendy and I were living in married housing at MSU, tucked into University Village. Football players on full scholarships weren't allowed to work while school was in session—NCAA rules—but we were given jobs during breaks. One winter, I was assigned to drive a delivery truck for Stroh's beer, making rounds to various bars and restaurants.

Drinking while driving was technically illegal, but in those days, no one paid it much mind. We were even encouraged to "be sociable within reason." But what exactly did "within reason" mean? I was quick to test the limits. By the end of each day, I was practicing my own version of "driving under the influence." The bartenders and regulars loved to chat with the guy from the MSU football team, always curious about the next game or the latest from the field. They'd buy me a round, and I'd stay, drinking with them, talking football, enjoying the easy acceptance that came with my jersey.

It was an early taste of something that felt powerful, almost invincible. I was young, strong, popular, and, more dangerously, oblivious to the path I was laying down for myself. Being sociable, I thought, was part of the job, a way of keeping everyone happy. But what I didn't see then was that I was building habits that would soon control me more than I'd ever control them. I was becoming my own best customer, unknowingly working toward a dependency that went well beyond "being sociable."

Looking back, I can see that the signs were there even then. I was drawn to the approval, the attention, the drinks—it all blended into one big, intoxicating rush. I didn't know it yet, but I was on my way down a path that would teach me more about limits, loss, and learning to surrender than any football game ever could.

CHAPTER SIX

THE REFEREE:
ESTABLISHING BOUNDARIES

My dad was young when I came into the world, just out of high school in the forties. I was born in 1949, and by the time I reached adulthood, he'd grown into his role, but some distance always lingered between us. Now, in the Alano Club meetings I attend, I find myself surrounded by military veterans, many from Vietnam, and I appreciate hearing their stories and insights. Some of them carry visible and invisible wounds from that time. Conversations with them offer a perspective I couldn't have had back then, but that resonates deeply now.

Being a college student in the late '60s was like stepping into a storm—racial tensions, Vietnam protests, and everything else swirling around campus. Woodstock was on the horizon, the Detroit Tigers had won the World Series, and my junior year saw the very first Earth Day. Tear gas hung in the air as regularly as campus bells tolled. I wouldn't trade those days for anything, as they taught me resilience, independence, and, strangely enough, a growing appreciation for the balance I'd later crave in sobriety.

One of the most memorable encounters I had years later was with a wrestling referee, a man awarded the Medal of Honor for his bravery as a medic in Vietnam. He was a conscientious objector who had been wounded twice on duty, and his story hit me deeply, reminding me of the sacrifices people make, often in silence. I thought about him when he officiated a wrestling match where one of my high school wrestlers won the Class A state championship.

Reflecting on those college years now, I see how they shaped me, gave me a sense of purpose, and instilled a willingness to question everything, even myself. Sobriety has brought me back to some of these memories, showing me how every experience, every protest, and every unlikely friendship formed part of a broader journey. The protests, the sports, the personal conflicts—they were all training grounds of sorts, preparing me for the challenges I would later face in recovery.

T. SHERMAN 2024!

Recently, a friend who'd been wounded in Vietnam shared something that struck me. He'd noticed that many men, just a bit too young for World War II, seemed to carry a strange regret, almost a guilt, for not having fought. He thought it was some form of "macho regret"—a feeling of having missed out on proving themselves. My father may well have been one of those men, shaped by that same gnawing feeling. Machismo, after all, seemed to be his middle name. The idea of surrender, let alone surrendering to addiction, would have been laughable to him. To him, surrender was weakness, plain and simple.

My father taught me that the most important thing in any situation was to be the toughest SOB in the room. He drilled it into me, a lesson reinforced time and again. It was the kind of mindset that left no room for vulnerability, no chance to step back and reconsider. How could I, raised in that world, ever see surrender as a step forward?

When I was in elementary school, the only time I was bullied was by an older kid. I told my parents about it, and my dad's response was instant and firm. He insisted I go back to school, find that kid, and kick his ass. And that's exactly what I did. Trouble? There'd be none of that from my dad's end. That day solved the immediate problem, but it left something behind—a reputation. From that point on, I was the kid you didn't mess with, and that reputation followed me, cementing the idea that toughness meant respect.

That single event marked the beginning of a decades-long identity. I became known as a badass, and with that came an unspoken rule: surrender was for cowards and weaklings. Life, as I saw it, was about facing challenges head-on, overpowering them, and never backing down.

But years down the line, when addiction crept in, I learned that surrender wasn't what I'd thought. Recovery asked something of me that felt like betrayal of my father's lessons. It required me to let go, to step back, to admit that I wasn't in control. That was the hardest fight I ever had to face—one that couldn't be won by brute strength, force, or reputation. It took me years to realize that true strength sometimes lies in letting go, in setting aside the need to be the toughest and embracing the humility of acceptance.

Sobriety taught me that surrender isn't about weakness; it's about wisdom. It's knowing when to push forward and when to step back. It's about choosing life over the illusion of strength, a lesson I never could have learned with my fists.

At 75, I still keep an eye on my temper. Old habits die hard. All through high school, college, and even the NFL, I carried this unshakable belief: I was the toughest guy on the field, maybe even in the room. That feeling was my armor, and it gave me a rush that I kept chasing, whether it was a clean hit on a football field or a solid drive on the golf course. Hell, I even fought in the Golden Gloves just for fun as a freshman. This wasn't just a pastime—it was a part of me, a way of life.

But looking back, I see the seeds of something else. Growing up, I'd come home after each game and sit at the kitchen table while my dad cracked open a beer and ran through every play. For every free throw I missed, every tackle I failed to make, he had something to say. In his way, he was training me, toughening me up, but I'm not sure he knew the cost. I suppose that kitchen table was as much a battlefield as any field I'd ever play on. I can still hear his voice, reminding me that good wasn't enough—greatness demanded a little extra, as Biggie Munn always said.

In a way, those post-game critiques became the bedrock of my success. I didn't need trainers or travel leagues; I had my dad's relentless drive pushing me forward. For him, life was a constant battle, and winning meant survival. Surrender wasn't in his vocabulary, and he made sure it wasn't in mine either. The motto was simple: show no weakness. But that same lesson, so valuable in competition, nearly became my undoing in recovery. I'd built my life on toughness, on pushing through no matter the odds. And yet, facing addiction required something different—something like surrender, which went against everything I'd been taught.

Now, looking back at the years, I realize that while strength had gotten me far, it was letting go—accepting my limits—that finally set me free.

In today's world, "stop bullying" has become a rallying cry, but I wonder if we're missing something by simplifying it so much. Bullying isn't always an isolated action; it often intersects with the ways we're taught to cope—or not cope—with life's tougher moments. For me, the lessons I learned growing up about strength and resilience became tied to my addiction, making the idea of surrender almost unthinkable.

I was raised in a way that left no room for softness. Surrendering was for the weak, and that mindset was drilled into me. Yet, ironically, finding sobriety has demanded that same surrender. I see this same challenge in many of my friends who are veterans. Like me, they've built their lives on the foundation of resilience, a trait that served them on the battlefield but turned into an obstacle in their recovery.

For my father, and then for me, strength meant never showing vulnerability. He held tightly to the notion that being the strongest in the room was the ultimate goal, passing down a mentality that would later clash hard with my journey to sobriety. Growing up, there was never a space to let down my guard, to admit that sometimes I couldn't handle it all. Surrender was an idea so foreign that I didn't even know how to begin.

Sobriety, however, isn't about conquering addiction in the way you'd take a hill or win a game. It's about something deeper—finding the strength to let go. That has been my toughest lesson yet, a lifelong struggle to unlearn what I'd been taught, to trade a badge of toughness for one of quiet resilience.

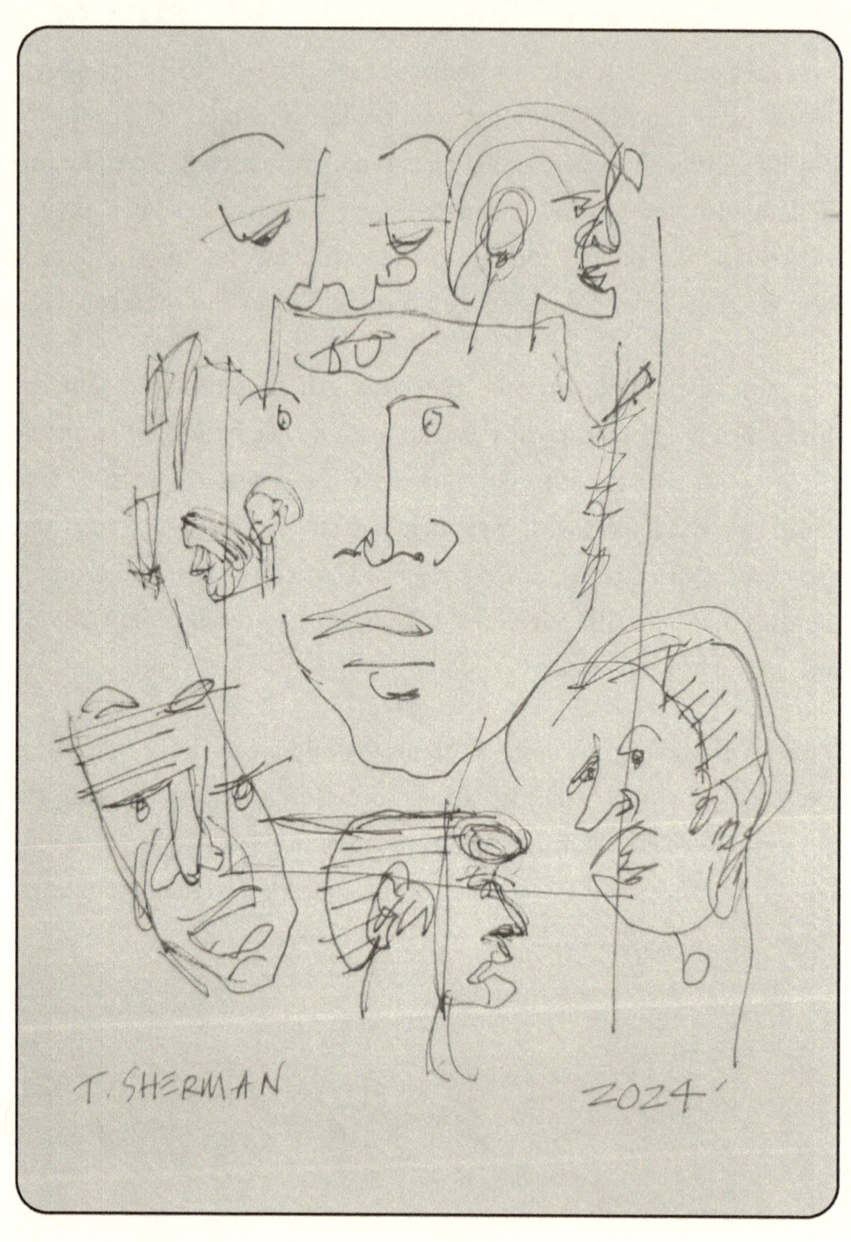
T. SHERMAN
2024

Bullying is a pervasive issue affecting individuals across various contexts, from schools to workplaces. Effectively addressing and preventing it requires differentiating between bullying behaviors and an ingrained bully personality. Although related, they stem from different causes and manifest in unique ways.

Bullying behavior is defined by an intent to harm or exert power over others, taking many forms such as physical aggression, verbal harassment, social exclusion, and cyberbullying. Motivations can range from a desire for control, revenge, or social validation. For some, it's a learned defense mechanism—emulating aggression absorbed from hostile or aggressive environments. Family dynamics, peer influences, and societal norms shape one's likelihood to bully, with many individuals passing frustrations onto others in a harmful cycle.

Moreover, bullying often roots in insecurity. Low self-esteem and a need to dominate drive individuals to bully as an attempt to elevate themselves, particularly in competitive environments. Stressful situations can exacerbate this, leading individuals to lash out as a means of reclaiming control. Over time, for some, this behavior solidifies into a bully personality, where learned aggression becomes a habitual response.

Society can further reinforce bullying when aggression is celebrated or dismissed. Individuals in such environments feel emboldened to continue their behavior, knowing there will be few, if any, consequences. To truly curb bullying, we must recognize these underlying influences, promoting environments where empathy, accountability, and self-reflection are valued over dominance.

Understanding the roots of bullying requires a deeper look at behavior and personality dynamics. Not all bullying stems from the same motives, nor does it arise from a "bully personality" alone. For many, bullying is an expression of personal conflict, insecurity, or environmental influence rather than a trait ingrained in their identity.

This difference between a "bully behavior" and a "bully personality" is crucial. Bullying behavior often manifests as an attempt to control or retaliate, motivated by circumstances such as peer pressure, a need for social validation, or even as a misguided defense mechanism. In contrast, a bully personality suggests a more deeply ingrained pattern, shaped by life experiences, societal conditioning, and unresolved insecurities. This duality reflects a larger continuum between empathy and self-interest, where our motivations frequently blend, shifting according to personal struggles and the surrounding social environment.

As a society, we can encourage behaviors that prioritize empathy and understanding over aggression. By addressing both immediate actions and underlying psychological factors, communities can move beyond mere "anti-bullying" slogans to foster environments where conflict resolution and emotional intelligence are taught. Encouraging empathy, promoting supportive relationships, and providing education on conflict resolution are powerful steps toward mitigating bullying. Through these comprehensive efforts, we can create an environment where respect and positive interactions prevail, supporting healthier communities and offering everyone the tools to manage personal challenges more constructively.

The relationship between alcoholism and bullying is both complex and deeply rooted in behavioral patterns. Alcohol not only impairs judgment but also lowers inhibitions, often leading to impulsive, aggressive behavior. For some, alcohol can become a gateway to actions they might otherwise control—aggression, dominating conversations, or pushing boundaries in social settings. When these actions cross the line into bullying, they expose a deeper issue: the way alcohol can amplify hidden insecurities or unresolved frustrations, fueling behaviors that harm others.

Growing up in an environment where alcohol abuse is normalized adds another layer. Witnessing aggressive or controlling behavior associated with drinking can shape a young person's understanding of conflict and power dynamics, embedding these as "normal" responses to stress. For those of us who have experienced both sides—being impacted by and perpetuating aggression—unpacking these learned responses is as crucial as managing the addiction itself. The depth of these cycles reveals why simple directives to "stop bullying" miss the mark; they fail to address the entangled roots of addiction, aggression, and, ultimately, the journey toward self-awareness.

In recovery, confronting these learned patterns is challenging but essential. Recognizing the weight of our actions under the influence, making amends, and moving forward requires vulnerability—a trait that, ironically, my early conditioning taught me to avoid at all costs.

Selfishness, in its simplest form, is that impulse to place our own needs above all else, often ignoring the impact on others. For someone battling addiction, selfish behavior can be a form of survival, a way to secure the next drink, the next escape. It's easy to fall into the pattern of prioritizing one's own desires, even to the detriment of those who love and support us. This behavior isn't always a deliberate disregard; often, it's a survival instinct masquerading as self-preservation. It's part of the paradox of addiction, where self-interest can become self-destruction.

Empathy, however, has the potential to break through this self-centered survival mode. Neuroscientific research shows how empathy engages parts of the brain linked to bonding and understanding others' emotions. Empathy encourages us to step beyond our own needs and see the needs of others, not just as a soft feeling but as a force pushing us to action, to create change.

In recovery, learning to activate this empathy is key. It becomes the foundation of making amends, of seeing our own actions from another's perspective, and understanding the hurt we may have caused. Yet it's not just about feeling guilty; empathy is about rebuilding connections and giving those relationships space to heal, sometimes at our own emotional cost.

To foster a culture that actively counters bullying and alcoholism, we need concrete steps, empathy-driven solutions, and supportive systems in place. Here are five pivotal strategies:

1. **Education and Awareness**: Establishing educational programs in schools and workplaces can play a vital role in addressing both bullying and alcoholism. By raising awareness around the damaging effects of these behaviors, we can demystify the struggles they bring and reduce associated stigma. This awareness doesn't just benefit those directly impacted; it helps foster a culture where seeking help feels both accessible and supported.

2. **Counseling and Support Groups**: Providing safe, non-judgmental spaces for people dealing with alcoholism or the effects of bullying can create a much-needed lifeline. Individual counseling and group therapy enable participants to share their experiences, exchange coping mechanisms, and

gain encouragement from others who've walked a similar path. Support groups often work as a powerful "team" where each person's success becomes a shared achievement.

3. **Conflict Resolution Training**: Teaching conflict resolution and healthy communication skills helps individuals navigate disagreements without defaulting to aggression or bullying. Equipping people with these skills fosters a mindset that values understanding over dominance and empathy over power, reducing the likelihood of conflicts escalating into harmful behavior.

4. **Parental Involvement**: Parents have a critical role in recognizing and addressing signs of bullying and alcoholism early on. Engaging them in open discussions through workshops and support sessions can help them spot the signs, support their children through challenges, and break cycles of behavior that could otherwise be handed down to the next generation.

5. **Peer Support Programs**: Initiating peer mentoring and support programs can empower students or employees to become allies in one another's well-being. Trained peers can help others cope with bullying or alcoholism by offering a familiar ear and supporting healthy behaviors. Such networks encourage people to lean on each other for strength and show that no one has to face these challenges alone.

Through these steps, we can build a framework for healthier, more supportive communities—ones where kindness and understanding replace aggression, and individuals are encouraged to find strength in both support and surrender.

It was only years later, through studying Buddhism, that I began to understand the strength required to truly surrender. For the first time, surrender wasn't a weakness; it was a courageous act, a choice to put down the armor I had carried my whole life. Looking back, I see how much of my journey would have been different had I learned that lesson sooner.

My older daughter, who lives in Athens, Georgia, had mentioned a friend of hers, a Native American author who owned a unique bookstore in Minneapolis. After moving to western Wisconsin, I made it a point to visit. One afternoon, I found myself in this cozy, eclectic bookstore, shelves full of wisdom and stories waiting to be uncovered. Browsing through the aisles, I stumbled upon a section dedicated to Buddhist recovery. I had no idea such a thing existed, but one of the titles caught my attention; it mentioned a list of recovery groups, and curiosity got the better of me.

Flipping through, I found a listing for Buddhist recovery meetings— one held in Kalamazoo, Michigan, where I was living at the time and attending AA. It was like a quiet invitation from the universe, one I was finally ready to accept. I began to attend those meetings, and in that space, I discovered perspectives I'd missed in my younger years. I left the bookstore that day with an armful of books, diving into Buddhist teachings and ancient wisdom that I had been too hardened, too stubborn, to explore before.

Studying these texts, I found that the concept of surrender had been in front of me all along—it just took this shift to see that surrender didn't mean giving up. It was letting go of the need to control everything, a release that offered a different kind of strength, a path towards a peaceful, sober life.

I learned to meditate, to focus on my breath, and to become more in tune with the present moment. As I explored this path, I found several spiritual teachers who encouraged me to create my own rhythm in recovery—my own path. Gradually, I set aside a specific time each night for introspection, a quiet space between my first and second sleep. "Eat when hungry, sleep when tired," became more than advice; it was a philosophy that helped me tune in to what my body and spirit actually needed.

My recovery journey expanded beyond the familiar walls of AA meetings, as I attended Buddhist recovery groups, both in the United States and abroad. Prince Edward Island, for instance, had groups that struck me with their honesty and warmth. Through these experiences, I began attending other spiritual and secular recovery meetings, discovering how different traditions address addiction with a shared, profound understanding.

One of the most powerful lessons I learned was this: desire transforms into craving, and craving, when left unchecked, becomes addiction. This sequence became clear in every story, every reflection shared in those meetings. While complex in the emotions it stirs, the path from desire to addiction is straightforward—and unraveling it begins with awareness.

My journey led me to explore both the familiar steps of Alcoholics Anonymous and the distinct Buddhist approach to recovery. The two share the same goal of sobriety, but their paths differ profoundly. In AA, the emphasis is on shared experience, reliance on community, and surrender to a Higher Power, a team effort with accountability. Buddhism, however, invited me to walk my journey in solitude, to seek freedom not just from substances but from attachments of all kinds.

Mindfulness, for instance, became the foundation of my Buddhist recovery. By focusing on the breath and observing my thoughts, I began to notice cravings as they arose and receded, learning to watch them without reacting—a skill AA doesn't necessarily emphasize but one that felt transformative in my own path. I began to understand the roots of suffering more clearly, recognizing that it's not just the substance that traps us but our cravings for it, our need to cling to what's fleeting.

Buddhism also taught me compassion—something I hadn't considered essential in my early recovery but which, in time, became one of my strongest tools. Through self-compassion, I began to soften the hard lines I'd drawn against myself, seeing my struggles with addiction not as weaknesses but as facets of my humanity. This non-attachment allowed me to see cravings as temporary, as transient whispers rather than demands. The Buddhist approach made it possible to envision sobriety as part of a broader, deeply personal spiritual journey, one where emotional resilience and acceptance paved the way.

I continued to cultivate these practices, building resilience not just to addiction but to the thoughts and cravings that triggered it. Rather than pushing them away or attempting to control them, I learned to sit with them. Practicing presence helped me cultivate a sense of gratitude, focusing on what I had rather than what I felt was missing. Through this journey, I learned that cravings stem from desire, which grows into attachment, and ultimately addiction. The process is simple, but not easy.

My journey to let go of attachments was just as essential as my journey to let go of addiction. I began to see that clutter, whether physical or emotional, often fed into attachment. To declutter my space and rely less on material items became a means of freeing my mind, creating room for clarity and peace. In the same way, learning to accept that experiences, people, and feelings are transient grounded me in the present moment, something that initially felt unsettling but ultimately became a source of comfort.

I started to establish healthier boundaries, understanding that my wellbeing depended on balancing my need for connection with my ability to stand on my own. Trying new activities and meeting new people shifted my focus, drawing me away from attachments that no longer served me and opening my mind to fresh experiences.

Through this process, I learned that it was essential to be kind to myself, recognizing that letting go is a gradual and often challenging process. I came to accept that the strength to release attachments would come from patience and consistent, compassionate effort. Embracing the steps one by one, I found that decluttering, both mentally and physically, freed me to cultivate emotional freedom and resilience.

Attachments—whether to people, possessions, beliefs, or outcomes—can deeply impact our emotional well-being. Learning to recognize and gently release these connections can help foster resilience and a greater sense of peace. Here are some practical steps for examining and addressing attachments:

1. **Identify Your Attachments**

   Start by recognizing what or whom you are attached to. This could include people, possessions, beliefs, or outcomes.

2. **Observe the Emotions Tied to Attachments**

   Pay attention to how you feel about these attachments. Notice any emotions that arise when you imagine losing them.

3. **Question the Root of Attachment**

   Ask yourself questions like: What needs does this attachment fulfill? What fears do I have about losing it? How does it shape my identity or self-worth?

4. **Reflect on Past Experiences**

   Consider how past experiences—childhood, relationships, life events—may have influenced these attachments.

4. **Examine Your Beliefs and Values**

   Are there beliefs that make certain attachments seem essential for happiness or self-worth?

5. **Write Down Your Reflections**

   Journal your thoughts to clarify emotions and detect patterns that may not be obvious initially.

6. **Seek Insight from Others**

   Share your reflections with a trusted friend or therapist who can offer fresh perspectives.

7. **Consider Letting Go**

   Gradually expose yourself to the idea of loosening these attachments. Observe how it feels to detach slowly.

8. **Practice Mindfulness**

   Use mindfulness to observe your thoughts and feelings without judgment. This helps you view attachments as external to your core self.

9. **Repeat the Process Regularly**

   Revisit this process as you grow. Attachments and their significance will change, offering new insights as you evolve.

By examining and loosening our attachments, we open the door to greater emotional freedom and peace, letting go of unnecessary suffering and embracing a more mindful approach to life.

CHAPTER SEVEN

THE TEAM CAPTAIN: ONE PLAY AT A TIME

MY JOURNEY WITH ATTACHMENT TOOK AN UNEXPECTED turn during three unforgettable moments at PGA major tournaments. In golf, the ability to let go of an unusually bad or exceptionally good shot is essential; a distracted mind is an ungrounded one. I had a front-row seat to these legendary moments—ones that still echo in the halls of golf history—and each reminded me of the importance of release and resilience, especially in the high-stakes atmosphere of competition.

The first of these defining moments happened in the 1985 U.S. Open at Oakland Hills Country Club, near Detroit, Michigan. My wife and I were there with friends, and on that Sunday, I felt the urge to stretch my legs and explore. TC Chen, who was leading the tournament that day, was on the fourth hole. I stood no more than thirty feet away, close enough to feel the tension in the air, when he made a costly mistake. In what felt like a surreal slow-motion moment, Chen's chip shot from the apron struck his club twice—a mishap that immediately attracted a penalty under golf rules at the time. In that brief, unforgettable instant, I was reminded of how easily one moment can disrupt an entire path, teaching us the invaluable art of detachment and the importance of moving forward.

As I stood there, so close to the unfolding event, it became clear that attachment—whether to victory, performance, or even a momentary mistake—could be as much a trap as it is a motivator. This lesson, felt up close through an extraordinary series of coincidences, has been invaluable in understanding the power of letting go and the resilience needed to thrive amid setbacks.

Observing iconic moments on the PGA tour firsthand has taught me invaluable lessons about the power of detachment and the necessity of maintaining focus. In golf, as in life, the ability to release attachment—whether to a mistake or a moment of triumph—is essential. One moment's hold on our minds can derail an entire journey. These experiences at historic tournaments underscored this truth.

Minutes later, as I strolled toward the clubhouse, I paused by the ninth hole tee box to watch Ben Crenshaw. In contrast to Chen's struggle, Crenshaw executed a flawless hole-in-one on the 235-yard hole—a single, immaculate shot. Witnessing these moments back-to-back brought home the immense mental resilience needed to play golf at the highest level. Just as a brilliant shot can propel you forward, a painful error can drag you down unless you can let it go. This delicate balance of attachment and detachment is at the heart of every success story.

Fast forward to the 2011 Masters Tournament at Augusta National, where I encountered a similar lesson. I had left my chair near the tenth green during the final round, trusting that it would remain undisturbed (an honored tradition at Augusta). When I returned, Rory McIlroy was stepping up to the tenth tee, leading the tournament as he turned onto the back nine. His drive, however, landed off course, and his second shot veered further left, lodging in a low valley near the green. His third shot hit the bunker on the right—a treacherous downhill position. The resulting double bogey was just the beginning of a challenging back nine for McIlroy. Watching it unfold, I was reminded again that attachment—to a shot, an outcome, or a lead—can blur the focus needed for each new moment.

These experiences reminded me that every shot, like every moment in life, must be treated with a balance of commitment and detachment. Being a witness to these long-shot events taught me that, despite the odds, sometimes things line up to bring you face-to-face with lessons you're meant to learn.

My journey with sobriety has taught me that, like golf, it demands resilience and a well-practiced ability to let go. Standing just feet away from history-making golf shots, I saw firsthand how both triumph and setback hinge on a player's ability to detach from the outcome of any single moment. This lesson remains crucial in the game of life, particularly for those of us who grapple with addiction.

The 2011 Masters at Augusta offered a vivid example. Rory McIlroy was leading as he teed off on the back nine's tenth hole. Watching from my seat beside the tenth green, I saw Rory's drive go wide into the trees. His second shot veered left, ending in the valley, and a bunker shot finally rolled well past the hole. The double bogey that followed shattered his rhythm, ultimately leading to a 15th-place finish—a plunge on the leaderboard that all began with one stray drive. Rory's "second arrow" that day was a costly loss, all stemming from a single error that spiraled out of control. Letting go of mistakes, it turns out, is often harder than correcting them.

The preceding year, I watched Phil Mickelson turn a near-miss into mastery on the 13th at Augusta, where he found himself off the fairway, stuck in pine straw behind a row of trees. Most would have laid up, but Phil had other plans. With audacious confidence, he took out his long iron, hooked the ball through the trees, and landed it three feet from the hole for an eagle. That choice became the pivot point for the final round, leading him to his third green jacket. I had the privilege of standing behind him during that miraculous shot—a shot that is now marked with a bronze plate at Augusta. For Phil, his "second arrow" transformed into triumph because he chose to move beyond the setback of his first.

Moments like these offer reminders that we all carry our own version of "the second arrow" in life. The concept, drawn from Buddhism, is that the first arrow represents unavoidable pain, like a missed shot or setback. The second arrow, however, is our choice—how we respond, whether we let the initial pain grow into suffering, or let it go. Maintaining that mindset—whether on the green or in the everyday challenges of sobriety—becomes our ongoing practice.

Golf is heralded as a game of integrity—a place where honesty isn't just encouraged; it's expected. In my sixty years of playing, I've witnessed nearly every type of rule violation, some out of ignorance, but often quite intentional. It's a unique culture: a sport where the rules are sacred, yet many players find themselves bending them. And for individuals grappling with alcoholism, there's often an extra layer to this behavior, rooted in addictive tendencies and impaired judgment.

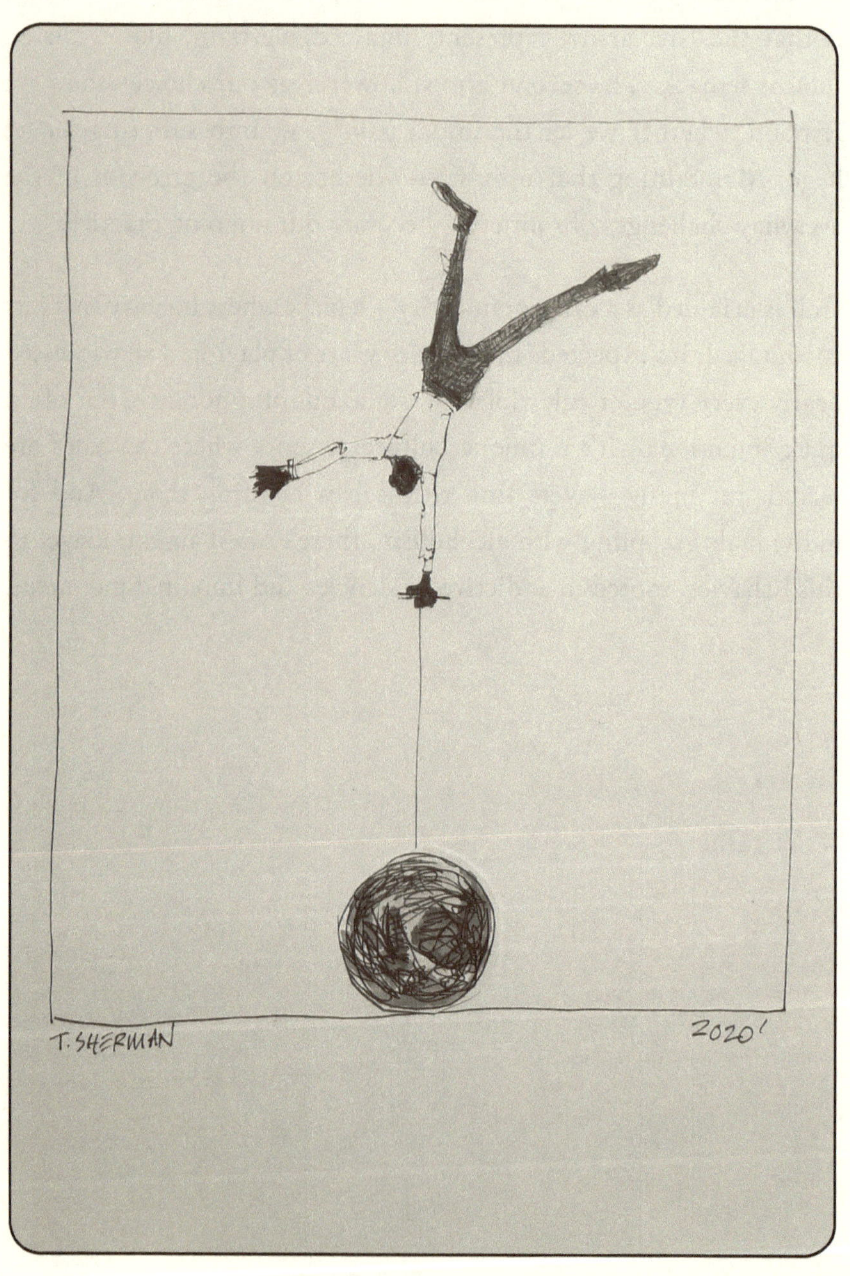

T. SHERMAN
2020'

The nature of addiction often distorts one's sense of right and wrong, and in a game like golf, where self-regulation is the foundation, this can manifest in subtle ways. Alcoholism, in particular, impairs the cognitive functions that guard integrity—judgment, impulse control, and even a sense of personal responsibility. Under the influence, a person might rationalize a minor rule bend as harmless or necessary in the moment, unaware of how addiction is rewriting their own playbook.

Some might wonder why an alcoholic would risk tarnishing the honor code that golf demands. It's an essential question, revealing a profound struggle between the desire for integrity and the shadow of addiction. In recovery, acknowledging these slips is vital, as is understanding the internal justifications that once seemed reasonable. Sobriety teaches us that the path forward involves clarity—like that required of a player who, after bending the rules, must look themselves in the mirror. Recovery demands we hold ourselves accountable, not only on the course but in life, respecting the "rules" of honesty, transparency, and self-awareness.

Golf's paradox is that it calls for absolute honesty, yet offers countless opportunities to stray. My journey toward sobriety has mirrored this: a practice of integrity, clarity, and restraint—qualities cultivated both in the game of golf and in the pursuit of a life free from the cloud of addiction.

The influence of alcohol can distort reality, where the immediate thrill of a win can overshadow the underlying principles of fair play. For individuals battling alcoholism, impaired judgment and warped perceptions often take hold, allowing actions that might seem uncharacteristic when sober. Addiction frequently reshapes personal ethics, skewing moral compasses that would otherwise steer toward honesty.

Golf, for many, is a temporary sanctuary—a space to escape personal issues. In this setting, cheating can emerge as a means to alleviate the stress of reality. By bending the game's rules and reveling in a false sense of accomplishment, alcoholics may feel a fleeting relief from their struggles. But this escape is short-lived, eventually feeding into a cycle of guilt and shame that compounds the destructive habits of addiction.

For those addicted, the sport's inherently competitive spirit and ego-driven moments can lead to actions misaligned with the game's values of integrity and sportsmanship. Cheating, whether through self-deception or the pressure of competition, serves as a fleeting balm. Yet, understanding these motivations provides insight not only into the behavior itself but also into how the environment can foster honest accountability.

Promoting healthier coping mechanisms, as well as social interactions that reflect the true spirit of golf, becomes essential. For golfers and those in recovery alike, aligning oneself with principles of integrity transforms both the game and the life played beyond the fairway. By fostering a space where honesty is celebrated, golf offers more than a game; it offers a practice ground for resilience, humility, and authenticity that can extend well beyond the course.

The time, location, and day of the week add unique flavors to each group meeting, with every variation holding a special role for those seeking sobriety. For many, this "Group Of Drunks" serves as their higher power. Weekday morning meetings, for instance, often attract older, retired, and strikingly joyful individuals—many of whom seemed, to my younger self, inexplicably happy. I would look around and wonder, "What on earth are they so damn happy about?" But today, I see them as living testaments of what we were, what happened, and what we are now.

Recently, I listened to an interview with Joe Namath. In it, he shared that his first thirteen years of sobriety were spent as a "dry drunk"—not drinking, yet not fully surrendering to recovery. Too embarrassed to enter rehab or attend AA, he endured without addressing the core of his addiction. It was only later, as he embraced surrender, that he found his current peace and happiness. His story resonates deeply with my own path, reminding me that recovery isn't merely abstaining; it's about the journey to wholeness and true joy.

Evening, weekend, and late-afternoon meetings often attract a diverse crowd, including many new faces who are visibly nervous and unsure. First meetings are tentative, sometimes intimidating, and many people might feel these meetings aren't for them. There's an imaginary barrier that can make entering these spaces difficult, especially for newcomers. I often suggest to people to "try different meetings and meeting places until you find one that's comfortable."

New members are encouraged to "take it one day at a time" and to "keep coming back," as both are foundational mantras within the group. This Group Of Drunks (GOD) becomes a lifeline for many—a higher power within the camaraderie of shared struggle. Sometimes, it takes multiple attempts before someone feels ready to return. The idea of surrendering to a "Higher Power" also puts people off at first. Yet, simply white-knuckling through these initial barriers, with patience and openness, can lead to a personal understanding of POWERLESSNESS that lays the foundation for healing.

In many ways, the journey to sobriety begins by establishing a routine—showing up, listening, and letting the process unfold. I've seen people develop self-awareness, practice self-regulation techniques, and find a pathway through their cravings by sitting in these rooms, week after week, and giving it a chance.

Some people only come to listen, learn, and turn things over to their chosen "Higher Power" until they understand their place in the larger picture. Timm Anderson once said, "My GOD had to be reincarnated eight times," a reminder that everyone's path looks different. For some, recovery involves developing a relationship with a chosen spiritual guide, while others focus on inner growth. In all cases, there is power in the collective, in the act of showing up, and in allowing oneself to lean on the support offered in the group setting.

Cravings are relentless. Ignored, they don't simply disappear; instead, they strengthen, digging deeper roots into our psyche. We reach a point where WE WANT WHAT WE WANT, AND WE WANT IT NOW. This yearning can feel almost unstoppable, pushing us toward what seems like instant relief. But cravings are not mere passing desires—they lay the groundwork for something far more consuming.

Unchecked, these cravings evolve into full-blown addiction. Addictions are learned behaviors, deeply ingrained through repetition, with each moment of satisfaction reinforcing the cycle. What may start as a simple craving quickly escalates into a routine of compulsive behavior, one that grows more sophisticated and persistent as it feeds on itself. It's a process fueled by the brief buzz of satisfaction, a fleeting relief that temporarily quells the craving but ultimately deepens the need.

This is the nature of addiction: a more advanced form of craving, where every fulfilled desire only strengthens the chains that bind us, feeding the craving that now drives us. Recognizing this evolution is essential in our journey, as understanding the origins of our cravings can be a powerful tool in reclaiming control.

Addiction manifests as a powerful cycle, shaped by various factors that make breaking free feel nearly impossible. Here's a closer look at the elements that drive this cycle and complicate recovery efforts:

1. **Loss of Control**: Addiction is marked by an initial struggle with control that escalates into a complete loss of it. Despite the negative impacts, people find themselves drawn repeatedly to the same behaviors—whether substance use, gambling, or unchecked anger. This repetitive cycle of losing control and seeking relief from life's challenges becomes a daily, undesirable existence.

2. **Tolerance and Escalation**: Over time, individuals develop a tolerance to the addictive behavior or substance, needing more to achieve the same effect. This escalating cycle leads to increased consumption, compounded by withdrawal symptoms when the behavior is interrupted. The distressing nature of these symptoms reinforces the compulsion, drawing the individual back into the cycle.

3. **Preoccupation**: Addiction takes over one's thoughts, becoming a constant fixation. Those affected spend much of their time planning, obtaining, and engaging in the addictive behavior, causing them to neglect relationships, responsibilities, and activities that once brought meaning to their lives.

4. **Negative Consequences**: The toll of addiction reaches every aspect of life: physical health, mental well-being, relationships, and work all suffer. Even as addiction brings severe consequences and threatens lives, the overpowering cravings drive people back, underscoring the challenging nature of the journey to sobriety.

5. **Compulsion**: The strong, almost irresistible urge to engage in addictive behavior fuels the cycle. These compulsions create a sense of urgency that makes ignoring cravings feel unbearable, further entrenching individuals in the cycle of addiction.

In some instances, **Legal Requirements for Sobriety** add another layer to the complexity. Court-ordered sobriety can be a stipulation in cases of DUIs, child custody battles, or even as a condition of employment in fields like healthcare. While these measures aim to promote public safety and personal well-being, many struggling with addiction find forced sobriety to be restrictive and sometimes unsustainable without genuine support.

Understanding the roots of this cycle reveals the broader impact of addiction on self-worth, relationships, and life's purpose. Emphasizing compassion, community, and consistent support through recovery is central in *Sobriety Is a Team Sport*—a journey of resilience, awareness, and hope in the face of life's most challenging patterns.

Addiction is a deeply layered condition that typically involves genetic, psychological, social, and environmental influences. Breaking free from its grip requires more than willpower; it's a journey that often demands a combination of support systems and self-reflection. For those who choose not to pursue recovery, the end of the road can be stark, often leading to consequences such as legal troubles, serious health impacts, or the inevitable need for intervention.

Here are foundational principles that can support individuals in overcoming addiction and embracing healing:

1. **Acknowledging the Problem**: The first step to recovery is acknowledging the presence of addiction and the inability to

control it. Denial can be one of the most significant barriers to healing. Understanding and accepting this reality are essential to making the necessary changes.

2. **Seeking Professional Help**: Alcohol rehabilitation centers, counseling, and therapy provide essential resources for those struggling with addiction. Support groups, like Alcoholics Anonymous (AA)—which began nearly 90 years ago as a small circle of individuals sharing their struggles—continue to offer community and connection as vital components of the recovery journey.

3. **Embracing the Challenge of Healing**: Recovery is not a one-size-fits-all process; however, it often requires a mix of personalized approaches, self-reflection, and accountability. The journey can be demanding, but support systems, professional help, and community-based programs can make all the difference in maintaining sobriety.

4. **Facing the Choices**: As much as recovery involves customized solutions, the list of potential outcomes for untreated addiction remains universal: jail, death, or the decision to heal. Recognizing these potential outcomes can create the urgency needed to seek help.

5. **Developing Self-Awareness**: Recovery involves building self-awareness and resilience against cravings. The internal struggles, habitual thoughts, and challenging emotions that lead to addiction require mindful attention. Developing tools for self-regulation, like mindfulness and stress-management techniques, strengthens individuals as they face their cravings head-on.

The process of overcoming addiction is intricate, but by prioritizing self-care, community, and structured support, individuals can find paths to stability and renewed hope. Through *Sobriety Is a Team Sport*, readers gain insight into the collective strength needed to overcome addiction, finding solidarity, empathy, and courage in the shared journey toward recovery.

The modern alcohol treatment center emerged out of the mid-20th century understanding that alcoholism is not merely a choice but a disease. Recognizing the physical and psychological components of addiction, society began to see the necessity of specialized treatment. Shortly after the founding of Alcoholics Anonymous in the early 20th century, the framework for formal centers developed, accelerating in the 1950s and 1960s as more comprehensive resources were established. This era marked a shift toward offering structured, therapeutic settings where individuals could find the medical and emotional support needed to overcome addiction.

Alcohol treatment centers provide a controlled environment to promote long-term sobriety. Through counseling, therapy, and a range of specialized programs, these facilities meet people where they are, equipping them to manage cravings and adopt new habits for a healthier future. While each center varies in its approach, many offer common components essential for recovery, such as:

- **Medical Detoxification**: Supervised, safe withdrawal from alcohol, managing withdrawal symptoms in a supportive setting.

- **Therapeutic Counseling**: Addressing the root causes of addiction, these programs foster emotional resilience and self-awareness.

- **Education and Skill-Building**: Learning about addiction's effects and developing tools to cope with life's challenges without substance reliance.

Sobriety is a journey, and specialized treatment centers represent a crucial pillar of support along that journey. Through facilities, community, and continuous learning, individuals can cultivate lasting change and discover a renewed sense of self, free from addiction.

Individual counseling—one-on-one sessions with a skilled therapist or counselor—can be pivotal in understanding and addressing the root causes of addiction. These sessions are designed to equip individuals with personalized coping strategies and insights, offering a confidential space to explore emotional triggers and create a path forward. For many, these intimate, focused conversations uncover the deeply personal motivations behind addictive behaviors, offering new perspectives and practical tools.

Yet, leaving the structured environment of a treatment center is only the beginning. Aftercare becomes the bedrock of lasting sobriety. The transition back into everyday life requires ongoing support and guidance, often through group meetings where shared experiences foster connection and accountability. Working through recovery steps can reveal layers of complexity, with certain steps requiring more assistance than others—a supportive community can make all the difference in staying the course.

As with any team sport, ongoing practice and support are essential to progress. Individuals are encouraged to explore various groups until they find one that resonates. Sobriety may begin as a solo journey, but it flourishes in community, where shared resilience, empathy, and encouragement become the ultimate sources of strength.

CHAPTER EIGHT

THE PLAYBOOK: PLAY SMART, WIN BIG

Through my years in AA, I've witnessed the crucial role that outside guidance plays in tackling the Fourth Step's often painful process of listing personal faults, fears, and past actions. This step—making "a searching and fearless moral inventory of ourselves"—asks individuals to dig deep, peeling back layers of shame and resentment that, for many, have fueled their addiction. It's a challenging step, especially the first time, as the impulse to hold back or gloss over difficult truths can be strong.

For newcomers, the initial Fourth Step list may feel incomplete. It was no different for me; my early lists barely scratched the surface. They were, admittedly, "half-assed," not because of laziness but because facing my past felt overwhelming. Over time, I learned that the Fourth Step isn't about getting it right the first time—it's about the willingness to look within, again and again if needed, to gain clarity and release the weight of unprocessed emotions.

Recognizing how tough this step can be, many AA groups offer workshops specifically designed to help members work through it. In these settings, sharing the struggle and understanding its purpose help make the experience less isolating. Guidance from others, including a sponsor, helps deepen the inventory and pushes us toward genuine self-examination.

Each Fourth Step list, no matter how uncomfortable, paves the way for growth. By revisiting and revising our lists, we continue to expand our self-awareness, allowing ourselves to identify destructive patterns and move forward. It's a process that requires courage but ultimately provides the foundation for personal transformation and lasting sobriety.

The Fourth Step in AA is an invaluable opportunity for growth, where we engage in deep self-examination and uncover paths toward healing. Here's a guide to help you navigate this pivotal step, embracing both the challenges and rewards it offers.

1) Be Honest

This step requires complete honesty. Face your behaviors and patterns with courage, allowing yourself to look at mistakes and imperfections without judgment. The courage to see things clearly is the first step toward meaningful change.

2) Make a List

Write down your resentments, fears, and any harmful behaviors you recognize. Take your time with each item, seeking to understand the underlying reasons for these emotions and actions. This isn't just a list; it's an exploration of your internal landscape.

3) Seek Guidance

Connect with your sponsor or a trusted person in your AA group for support. They can offer valuable insights, help clarify your understanding, and remind you that this step isn't meant to be faced alone.

4) Focus on Patterns

Observe recurring themes in your behaviors and relationships. Identifying these patterns can highlight areas that need attention and help you understand what triggers negative reactions, giving you a starting point for change.

5) Practice Self-Compassion

The purpose of the Fourth Step is not self-punishment but growth. Approach yourself with kindness. Remember, you're here to learn and evolve, not to dwell on guilt or shame. Compassion makes this process bearable and transformative.

6) Take Your Time

This step is a journey, not a race. Take the time to truly reflect on each part of your list, and don't rush. The slower pace allows for a more thorough, meaningful introspection, building a stronger foundation for what lies ahead.

7) Reflect on Your Strengths

While looking at your weaknesses, don't forget to acknowledge your strengths. Recognizing your positive qualities offers a balanced perspective, helping you see yourself fully. This balanced view provides motivation and helps build resilience.

This Fourth Step is about embracing self-discovery with courage, honesty, and patience. It's an invitation to look deeper into who you are, allowing you to grow beyond past challenges. Approach it with openness and the knowledge that change and healing are entirely within your reach.

The Role of Group Therapy in Recovery

Therapy sessions in a group setting are a cornerstone of the recovery journey, offering a sense of shared experience and camaraderie. Here, individuals find encouragement in one another's stories, realizing they are not alone in their struggles. These sessions foster a sense of community that extends beyond the treatment center and reinforces the idea that, in sobriety, support is essential.

In these sessions, participants gain access to valuable resources and education about alcoholism, addiction, recovery, and relapse prevention. This knowledge helps individuals understand their own conditions and equips them with the tools they need to make informed choices about their recovery.

Building Empathy and Self-Awareness

Through personal hardships, some individuals develop a strong capacity for empathy, recognizing the universal nature of suffering and the importance of compassion. Others, impacted by betrayal or neglect, may become more guarded, approaching life with a protective outlook that shapes their interactions and perspectives. Recognizing these diverse reactions to hardship can be transformative, shedding light on past behaviors and helping individuals approach recovery with both understanding and intention.

The Importance of Aftercare

Aftercare planning is essential for those leaving treatment centers, providing a personalized roadmap that supports their continued therapy journey. This step helps individuals transition back into their daily lives with confidence, armed with strategies and resources to maintain their sobriety. Alcohol treatment centers play a crucial role in this process, guiding individuals as they regain control and work toward a fulfilling, healthy future.

Recovery is a deeply personal journey but one that doesn't have to be taken alone. Healthcare professionals—therapists, counselors, or addiction specialists—provide essential support, helping individuals uncover the roots of addiction and develop personalized strategies to handle cravings and avoid triggers. These professionals are there to guide and support each step, making the journey toward sobriety a collaborative effort.

For some, the first phase of recovery includes detoxification, which can be medically supervised when necessary to manage withdrawal symptoms safely. Detox is a crucial step in preparing for the deeper work of emotional and psychological healing, providing a stable foundation from which individuals can begin to build healthier lives.

Therapy and counseling sessions—whether one-on-one or in a group setting—help individuals delve into the core of their addiction, identify negative patterns, and create healthier coping strategies. These sessions encourage self-awareness and resilience, empowering individuals to approach recovery with intention and strength.

Connecting with others who share similar struggles can be transformative, particularly within support groups like Alcoholics Anonymous (AA), Narcotics Anonymous (NA), or ACT. These groups offer a sense of belonging, fostering encouragement and accountability. For many, this shared connection becomes a powerful source of strength, often likened to a "higher power" that supports their commitment to sobriety.

Combining professional guidance, detox support, therapeutic counseling, and connection with peers provides a well-rounded foundation for a healthier, more fulfilling life in recovery.

Adopting a healthy lifestyle can become a pillar of recovery, offering structure, strength, and a fresh outlook. Building habits like regular exercise, balanced nutrition, good sleep, and stress management helps the body heal and creates a stable foundation for the mind to find balance. For some, medication-assisted treatment may also play a crucial role, supporting withdrawal, reducing cravings, or managing mental health challenges. Close collaboration with healthcare providers ensures a personalized approach, giving each person the best chance for recovery.

Support networks are essential, and often, it's those closest to us—family members, friends, a spouse—who provide the encouragement needed. I've been married for 56 years, which sounds like a lifetime even to me sometimes. We married young, still figuring out who we were, and then waited nearly a decade to start our family. Looking back, I wonder if I married early as a way to leave a family where love felt scarce. My wife's family, in contrast, showed love openly; I was drawn to it, fascinated by it. They welcomed me without hesitation, even as I adjusted to their warmth with a mix of gratitude and a bit of jealousy. My father-in-law owned a hardware store, played tenor sax, and loved sports. My mother-in-law took pride in her cooking, which I grew to love just as I grew to love her. I was fortunate, finding a second family that taught me to value closeness and embrace affection—something I might not have learned otherwise.

Building a support system goes beyond personal connections. It includes finding healthcare professionals, counselors, and even support groups that can provide guidance through recovery. Therapy sessions in group settings can offer a unique encouragement that comes from shared experiences, reminding each person that they're not alone in their struggles. Support groups like AA or Narcotics Anonymous, and others, foster community and accountability, and for many, they serve as a source of strength—a higher power of sorts—along the path to sobriety.

This journey is multifaceted, but with each layer of support, it becomes easier to envision a healthier and more fulfilling future.

Over time, my wife's family didn't just become family; they became our family. I'll admit I struggled with a mix of guilt and sadness about leaving behind my own younger sister and brother, knowing my relationship with them would inevitably shift. My parents had to adjust to the new reality of limited time together, but this wasn't without consequence. I felt for my mother, who would often be the one left out of moments with my kids. My daughters spent so much time with their maternal grandparents that, when it was time to leave, they'd cry. I felt for my mom, knowing they didn't seem to mind missing visits with her.

Reflecting on this dynamic has influenced my choices in retirement, particularly when we chose to move to my daughter's farm. Demonstrating love and presence for my grandchildren—being nearby to create memories and foster closeness—is a priority for me now. I want them to see what it looks like to be loved openly and consistently. Demonstrated love is the most powerful kind; it's love as a way of life, the kind I want modeled for my young grandsons.

The journey of understanding, both of others and ourselves, can reveal patterns we never anticipated. Recent research has shown that relationships involving empaths and those struggling with alcoholism appear more frequently than random chance would predict. These pairings are deeply complex, even challenging. An empath, who feels others' emotions as if they were their own, often stands as the ideal supporter yet faces unique vulnerabilities. Al-Anon might as well have been founded for them. This personality type is not only highly sensitive but can easily become codependent, making recovery and relationship health an ever-evolving challenge.

As my years of sobriety continue, I uncover more of these dynamics in the fabric of relationships, especially within family. Each layer we peel back in understanding reveals a little more about the roles we play, the patterns we inherit, and how they shape the paths we choose forward.

Alcoholism is a heavy force, casting a shadow over behavior, emotions, and relationships. When an empath finds themselves in a marriage with an alcoholic, the impact ripples through every layer of their connection. An empath feels not only their own emotions but also absorbs the struggles of those closest to them. As a partner to an alcoholic, they may become overwhelmed, trying to absorb their partner's pain while fighting to maintain their own strength. Despite an overwhelming urge to help, they can feel drained and emotionally depleted. In many cases, they find themselves slipping into codependent patterns, prioritizing their partner's needs over their own well-being, caught in the emotional storms of addiction.

These dynamics can quietly morph into a cycle where the empath enables the alcoholic's behavior—shielding them from consequences, excusing actions, or shouldering responsibilities that their partner cannot or will not meet. Communication in these relationships often becomes fraught and painful, marked by misunderstandings and conflicts born from denial and a lack of honest acknowledgment. For the empath, each emotional ripple in the relationship lands with the force of a wave, amplifying the intensity of these struggles.

I have come to understand how relationships, particularly those involving addiction, can reveal parts of ourselves and push us to confront the complexities within. The challenges for empaths in such partnerships are often overlooked, but they are no less significant.

Healing, for both individuals, requires support, self-compassion, and, ultimately, the strength to let go of cycles that neither serve nor uplift.

Over time, empaths who live with an alcoholic partner often develop emotional defenses to shield themselves from the chaos that surrounds them. These walls, though protective, can create a deep sense of isolation within the relationship. They struggle to maintain their own emotional well-being, frequently suppressing their needs in order to support their partner. But this approach leads to a heavy imbalance, where the empath is left carrying a burden not entirely their own, disconnected from the closeness they once felt.

Seeking outside support becomes vital, for both partners individually and together as a couple. Professional help offers a bridge between isolation and understanding. The alcoholic partner may benefit from therapy or specialized treatment to address the root of their addiction. At the same time, the empath has the opportunity to set boundaries, work on self-care, and learn how to offer support without sacrificing their own needs.

Healing in a relationship like this is possible, though it demands open communication, boundaries, and consistent support from professionals. Even once the alcoholic partner reaches sobriety, the dynamics of the relationship will inevitably shift—and not without challenges. Sobriety is a tremendous step forward, but it does not erase the emotional history between the couple. With time, patience, and commitment to growth, it's possible for both partners to find renewed balance and to build a future that honors both their needs.

The process of rebuilding a relationship after addiction is one of both hope and hard work. Sobriety can certainly bring clearer communication, allowing the couple to talk openly, perhaps for the first time in a long time, without the fog of addiction. The alcoholic partner, now sober, may be more present, genuinely able to listen and engage in conversations they once avoided. However, even as openness increases, trust remains a tender element to mend, and while trust can be rebuilt, history cannot be rewritten.

My wife's ultimatum from 1984 still stands as a pivotal moment in our lives. Her unwavering commitment gave me an anchor, a reminder that my actions carried consequences, even as the years and sobriety set in. Sobriety, though, is not a cure-all. The road forward demands ongoing dedication to heal the wounds created in both partners. With sobriety comes the opportunity for emotional healing: while the recovering alcoholic addresses the issues that contributed to their addiction, the empathic partner, too, focuses on their own well-being, working to overcome the impact of years spent in a chaotic and often painful environment.

Sobriety is a victory, a step in the right direction, but it also reveals new terrain. The changes that come with it can be complex and sometimes unsettling, almost like turning a pickle back into a cucumber—a notion as impossible as it sounds. The recovering alcoholic now has to navigate life without alcohol, facing emotional triggers and temptations head-on. The empathic partner, too, must adjust to this new person, finding ways to support without slipping back into old patterns of over-responsibility or emotional neglect.

Together, both partners have a chance to grow, to nurture a relationship based on real understanding and mutual respect. Though the journey forward is challenging, it's one that can bring about an authentic, lasting connection if both are willing to work toward it.In sobriety, a couple can work together, forging a path toward a healthier lifestyle and mutual growth. With the empath providing steadfast encouragement, understanding, and emotional support, and the recovering alcoholic dedicating themselves to sobriety and self-improvement, the partnership can deepen in meaning. Yet, sobriety does not mean all challenges will vanish; instead, both partners must actively nurture the relationship with open communication, boundary-setting, and a commitment to mutual respect, trust, and understanding. Acknowledging the past without letting it control the present is essential. The past should be remembered but left where it belongs.

The founders of Alcoholics Anonymous advised against forming a new romantic relationship in early sobriety due to the complications it could bring. Early sobriety is a time to prioritize personal growth, discovering one's own strengths and needs, and developing resilience. Building a solid sober network—a group of friends and supporters dedicated to sobriety—provides essential guidance and helps reinforce a commitment to this new path.

In time, sobriety can bring positive shifts in relationships, but new challenges will also arise. For both the empath and the recovering alcoholic, this journey is about enduring resilience, creating healthy boundaries, and cultivating a partnership grounded in shared dedication, respect, and love.

In sobriety, both partners must cultivate mutual respect and a deep understanding of each other's recovery journeys. A commitment to honest communication is essential, as is a willingness to set and respect boundaries around substance use and triggers. Sharing fears, aspirations, and challenges openly can lay a foundation of trust and understanding.

It's equally crucial for each partner to maintain personal independence and avoid becoming overly reliant on the other for emotional support. Each person must prioritize their own recovery practices and nurture a support network beyond the relationship. In early sobriety, relationships need time to develop naturally; rushing may introduce stress and risk to both partners' journeys.

For couples navigating recovery together, therapy or support groups specifically for couples can be instrumental. They provide a space for developing the skills needed to support one another without sacrificing individual growth. Staying committed to recovery means that sobriety must remain the top priority. If, at any point, the relationship begins to undermine one's recovery, it may be necessary to reassess its impact.

By following these practices, the couple can cultivate a relationship built on mutual support, strength, and understanding, allowing each partner to thrive individually and together on their recovery path.

Mindfulness can be a valuable practice for empaths, as it encourages them to stay fully present and observe their thoughts, emotions, and sensations without judgment. By focusing on the present moment, empaths can gain a clearer sense of their emotions versus those of others, helping them to react thoughtfully to challenging situations. In a similar way, compassion is central to maintaining a healthy recovery relationship. A teacher might encourage empaths to cultivate self-compassion, recognizing their own needs and limits, while also extending compassion toward those who may cause emotional strain. For empaths, maintaining these healthy boundaries and practicing self-kindness can be essential steps toward sustaining emotional well-being.

Healthy relationships are grounded in mutual well-being, and achieving this often requires each partner to embark on their own journey of growth. A teacher might encourage the empath to create boundaries that protect their emotional health. In Buddhism, practices like loving-kindness meditation—directing love and goodwill toward oneself and others—can help empaths cultivate a sense of peace, acceptance, and resilience. This practice can be particularly beneficial for empaths in recovery relationships, offering a calming anchor in moments of emotional turmoil.

For individuals in early sobriety, the advice to delay a new relationship has practical roots. Early recovery is a time for introspection and self-discovery, creating space for individuals to focus on their own needs and personal growth. Building a foundation of sober friendships and a supportive network can provide guidance during this period and help maintain sobriety.

Both addiction and codependency impact relationships deeply, often in ways we're unaware of until we look back and see the patterns. Just as the alcoholic requires guidance and tools to maintain sobriety, the codependent needs similar support to find their way to a healthier, more self-sustaining life. Groups like Al-Anon play a vital role in providing comfort, guidance, and a safe community for people facing codependency, helping them to share experiences and gain perspective.

For both the alcoholic and the codependent, mindfulness becomes essential. By being present and observing without judgment, individuals can recognize their own emotional needs and avoid becoming overwhelmed by the complexities surrounding addiction. This awareness fosters the resilience needed to respond to life's ups and downs with balance and clarity.

In Buddhism, the principle of impermanence reminds us that even the most difficult emotions are temporary and will eventually pass. A teacher might help one see that emotions can come and go like waves—powerful, but ultimately manageable. This perspective allows individuals to experience their emotions without becoming consumed by them, helping them to maintain balance even when life feels turbulent.

The phrase "born that way" often surfaces in addiction discussions, implying a fate bound by genetics or disposition. For me, it's always felt hollow—more of a catchphrase than a reality. When I hear it during the "How It Works" reading at an AA meeting, I struggle to recite it. And in this setting, questioning it outright isn't welcomed. But there's another perspective that is gaining ground: a view that recognizes both the biology and complexity of addiction without reducing it to a static label.

Emerging research on neurodiversity offers a more nuanced view of how people experience addiction. Conditions like autism, ADHD, or dyslexia, often included under the neurodiversity umbrella, are natural variations in human neurobiology. These variations deserve understanding, not stigma. Yet, for some neurodivergent individuals, managing the challenges of a society that may not align with their perspectives and needs can lead to an increased vulnerability to substance use disorders. Factors like social isolation, sensory processing difficulties, and challenges with impulse control contribute to this heightened risk.

Still, it's essential to recognize that not every neurodivergent person will face these challenges, and there is no one-size-fits-all experience in addiction. Each person has a unique journey shaped by a mix of their biology, environment, and experiences. The connection between neurodiversity and addiction is layered, varied, and complex, reflecting the full spectrum of human individuality. This understanding not only broadens our view of addiction but also opens up new ways of supporting those who might be at risk, creating room for empathy, tailored guidance, and respect for the diverse pathways people walk in life.

If you or someone you know is grappling with alcoholism or substance abuse, seeking help from healthcare professionals and supportive services is essential. Recovery can look different for everyone, and finding resources tailored to individual needs can be transformative. Many tools and approaches discussed here may provide a meaningful foundation for those seeking support on this path.

Discovering the teachings of Buddhism was, for me, like unearthing a hidden treasure. I'd expected wisdom, but I hadn't anticipated such a direct engagement with pain—one of Buddhism's central tenets. At the heart of its teachings is the idea that life's suffering isn't something to run from but something to observe and understand. These teachings felt like a reintroduction to mindfulness, and reading the ancient texts, I found myself reflecting on how profoundly they addressed struggles universal to human experience. The insights felt familiar, almost as if an ancient voice were validating the same practices we seek today to make peace with pain and cultivate resilience.

In bringing these ideas into recovery, I saw an opportunity: mindfulness isn't just a tool for sobriety; it's a way to embrace every aspect of the journey—its pain, progress, and moments of peace. And perhaps in doing so, we can come closer to a sense of freedom and acceptance that feels as grounding as it does timeless.

If you're seeking help with addiction, you may find unexpected guidance in Buddhism's Three Jewels. These Three Jewels, also known as the Three Refuges, form the core foundation of Buddhist practice and offer insights into healing and wholeness.

1. **The Buddha:** Siddhartha Gautama, the historical Buddha, achieved enlightenment and shared a path out of suffering. Taking refuge in the Buddha means choosing to trust in the possibility of transformation—trusting that change and liberation from suffering are within reach. The Buddha's journey shows that with courage and commitment, anyone can move toward peace and self-understanding.

2. **The Dharma:** This represents the teachings, such as the Four Noble Truths and the Noble Eightfold Path, which guide individuals on the path of wisdom and compassion. Taking refuge in the Dharma involves not only studying these teachings but also living them, bringing them into our daily lives and challenges. It means recognizing suffering without letting it define us—a powerful perspective for those on a recovery journey.

3. **The Sangha:** The Sangha is the community of practitioners, a supportive network on the spiritual path. For those in recovery, the Sangha could be found in your sobriety group, in the friends and mentors who walk with you, sharing experiences, insights, and encouragement. This community provides resilience and reminds us that we are not alone in our struggles.

For those on the path to sobriety, grounding oneself in these Three Jewels offers not only comfort but also a structured approach to resilience, reinforcing that the journey to inner peace is possible through wisdom, support, and compassion.

In group therapy, we learn through each other's stories and experiences. As we listen, a foundational trust emerges, allowing a shared understanding of addiction to deepen. Here, the roots of support grow from compassion and understanding, and we're reminded not to take "inventory" of each other's lives but to embrace each individual's journey.

In Buddhism, taking refuge in the Three Jewels embodies a similar commitment to growth. These Three Jewels—the Buddha, Dharma, and Sangha—offer guidance, strength, and a sense of community. The Buddha represents the journey toward enlightenment, serving as a source of inspiration and hope for anyone seeking freedom from suffering. The Dharma, or teachings, provides us with tools like the Four Noble Truths and the Noble Eightfold Path, guiding us to face suffering with openness. In addiction recovery, these teachings can be profound, offering clarity and helping us find peace within.

The Sangha, much like a support group, represents fellowship and shared experiences. It is in this community that we find encouragement and collective strength. In the context of recovery, the Sangha may be our fellow group members, each offering empathy, resilience, and an unwavering commitment to progress.

A Buddhist teacher might encourage us to look toward these Three Jewels as sources of guidance and stability, grounded in mindfulness, compassion, and wisdom. Through these principles, we're invited to build self-awareness, foster resilience, and embark on a journey of personal and spiritual growth.

In Buddhism, Mara is a powerful symbol, often depicted as a demon or embodiment of temptation and distraction. His role is to disrupt an individual's journey toward enlightenment by presenting desires, fears, and doubts—anything that might deter them from their path.

One of the most iconic encounters with Mara occurs as Siddhartha Gautama meditates beneath the Bodhi tree. Mara unleashes a series of temptations and threats, aiming to sway him, but Siddhartha remains resolute, ultimately achieving enlightenment. Mara represents the internal and external challenges we all face: attachment, ignorance, and the lure of worldly pleasures.

This notion of "facing Mara" resonates with the challenges on any transformative journey. Buddhist teachings often remind us of the "second arrow" analogy, a metaphor for how we add suffering to pain by resisting or clinging to it. The practice of confronting Mara—whether he appears as doubt, fear, or desire—invites us to approach these inner obstacles with clarity, mindfulness, and compassion. Just as Siddhartha did, we too can learn to confront and transcend these distractions, moving closer to our true purpose.

Self-care practices, mindfulness exercises, and relaxation techniques become invaluable tools on this path. They help cultivate inner peace and resilience, enabling us to face life's temptations with a grounded spirit. In Buddhism, this path is the journey toward Nirvana—a state of liberation from Samsara, the cycle of birth, death, and rebirth. By embracing this journey, we draw closer to enlightenment, finding peace amid life's inevitable challenges and achieving liberation from suffering.

Nirvana, the ultimate state of peace and liberation from suffering, embodies the cessation of desire and attachment—a goal achieved through spiritual practices, ethical living, and the development of wisdom and mindfulness. In Buddhism, it's the highest aim, leading to lasting happiness and freedom.

Recovery from addiction mirrors this transformative journey. The Twelve Steps of Alcoholics Anonymous (AA) and Buddhism's Three Remembrances offer complementary frameworks that guide individuals toward healing and self-awareness. While the Twelve Steps emphasize spiritual growth and personal responsibility, the Three Remembrances underscore mindfulness and the impermanence of life. The synergy between these two approaches provides a holistic path to recovery, focusing on overcoming addiction, nurturing a spiritual connection, and building a supportive community.

Key steps within the Twelve Steps—such as admitting powerlessness over alcohol, seeking a higher power, making amends, and helping others suffering from addiction—help individuals build resilience through honesty, humility, and service. The Three Remembrances, focusing on the inevitability of death, the transient nature of life, and the interconnectedness of actions (karma), deepen this journey, encouraging practitioners to reflect on suffering and the motivations that drive their actions.

Bringing these systems together reinforces the concept of interconnectedness, highlighting how personal actions impact not only oneself but also the wider community. This understanding of connection fosters compassion and motivates individuals to contribute positively to others' lives. Much like the AA fellowship, the Three Remembrances offer a lens through which individuals can recognize their shared struggles and the support available in community bonds.

In the AA process, Steps Eight and Nine—making amends and acknowledging past wrongs—echo the Buddhist concept of karma, emphasizing the importance of accountability and understanding the consequences of one's actions. This process isn't merely about seeking forgiveness but recognizing how behavior affects others, fostering healing, and paving the way toward reconciliation. By embracing these principles, individuals in recovery can find a balanced path forward, enriched with compassion, community, and personal growth.

In the later steps of Alcoholics Anonymous (Steps Ten through Twelve), the emphasis shifts toward ongoing self-reflection, spiritual growth, and service to others. This continuous cycle aligns with the Buddhist practice of mindfulness, which promotes self-awareness and fosters compassion for oneself and others. Practicing mindfulness allows individuals to stay present, acknowledge their struggles, and develop a compassionate attitude, forming a powerful framework for recovery. Integrating the AA Twelve Steps with Buddhist teachings like the Three Remembrances creates a holistic approach, addressing both the physical aspects of addiction and fostering spiritual and emotional growth.

This approach allows individuals to navigate their journey with clarity and purpose, embracing concepts such as powerlessness, interconnectedness, karma, and mindfulness. By integrating these practices, individuals find not only a path to sobriety but also strength in vulnerability, wisdom in impermanence, and hope in the shared experience of recovery. Such synergy encourages a more fulfilling, spiritually aligned life.

A portrayal of these themes appeared in the early 1990s TV show Northern Exposure, a series known for exploring interconnectedness, mindfulness, and the search for meaning in everyday life. The show emphasized community, accepting diverse perspectives, and the personal growth that comes from embracing life's unpredictability. Joel Fleischman, a New York doctor transplanted to small-town Alaska, wrestles with his own inner challenges as he seeks personal direction. His journey often mirrored Buddhist principles, with characters like the "demon" symbolizing his inner fears and anxieties.

These storylines and characters were a creative depiction of the complexities of human emotion and self-discovery, mirroring a real-life journey toward self-acceptance and compassion. This idea of facing one's "demons" and embracing one's inner struggles parallels the challenges of sobriety and personal transformation, reinforcing the belief that authentic growth comes from facing our fears with openness, awareness, and support from our community.

This framework of AA's steps and Buddhist principles empowers individuals to transform through mindfulness and interconnectedness, inspiring them to build a life rooted in clarity, compassion, and authenticity.

The journey of recovery is deeply personal yet profoundly interconnected with others. In the TV series *Northern Exposure,* themes of fulfillment and self-acceptance emerge as characters learn that true peace comes from within rather than seeking approval from others. This message resonates with Henri Nouwen's concept of the "Wounded Healer," which suggests that those who have faced and embraced their own wounds can offer genuine empathy and healing to others. For those on the path of recovery, vulnerability becomes a transformative force, as sharing one's struggles invites others to do the same, creating a foundation of trust and community.

The "Wounded Healer" concept highlights how embracing our own pain is vital for growth and connection. Recovery from addiction—like healing from any deep wound—demands patience, perseverance, and ongoing effort. As individuals confront their own suffering, they can foster authentic connections with others, offering a space where shared experiences bring mutual understanding and support. This dynamic is essential in recovery communities, where encouragement comes not from quick solutions but from listening, presence, and compassion.

In both Alcoholics Anonymous (AA) and Buddhism, the idea of healing is grounded in community and self-awareness. Steps Ten through Twelve in AA focus on self-reflection, spiritual growth, and service—similar to mindfulness practices in Buddhism, where staying present nurtures personal development and compassion. Integrating the AA Twelve Steps with Buddhist practices like the Three Remembrances creates a powerful framework for recovery. The Twelve Steps help individuals to address addiction, seek spiritual guidance, and foster community, while the Buddhist remembrances of death, impermanence, and karma encourage a reflective awareness of life's transient nature.

This synthesis of AA and Buddhist principles highlights interconnectedness. By recognizing that our actions impact others, individuals in recovery can find resilience through community and support, much like in AA fellowships. In Step Eight and Step Nine of AA, making amends to those harmed by one's actions echoes the Buddhist remembrance of karma, focusing on understanding the consequences of actions and fostering a path of healing and reconciliation.

Ultimately, these parallel philosophies suggest that true growth comes from looking inward, acknowledging vulnerability, and embracing the shared experience of recovery. Through self-reflection, community support, and spiritual practices, individuals find both healing and purpose on their journey toward a fulfilled and meaningful life.

CHAPTER NINE

THE INJURED PLAYER: SUPPORT & UNITY

I N RECOVERY, PROGRESS—RATHER THAN PERFECTION—SERVES
as the ultimate goal. Embracing small victories becomes essential,
as these triumphs remind us that healing, while challenging, is
possible through commitment, support, and the courage to change.

Along this journey, the concept of surrender plays a powerful role.
It's easy to feel the sting of sarcasm from others, as in, "So, how's that
Buddhism thing working out for you?" Yet the strength to surrender
lies not in responding to doubt, but in finding peace within ourselves.
Here are ways to cultivate this skill, even in difficult situations:

1. **Acceptance:** Embrace the reality that not every aspect of
   life is controllable. Acceptance isn't about giving up; it's
   about knowing where your power lies, as the Serenity Prayer
   reminds us.

2. **Self-Compassion:** Be gentle with yourself. Letting go of the
   need for control and perfection is not a sign of weakness but
   of self-respect.

3. **Mindfulness:** Practicing mindfulness helps you observe your inner experiences without judgment, cultivating awareness of your thoughts and emotions, enabling you to make decisions rooted in clarity.

4. **Trust:** Develop trust—in yourself, in life's process, and in the support system around you. Remember, surrender is a step toward growth and healing, letting things unfold as they are meant to.

5. **Seek Support:** Reach out to trusted friends, family, or mentors. Sharing your journey can lift emotional burdens and offer fresh perspectives.

6. **Release Ego:** Letting go of ego-driven desires and expectations allows humility and a greater sense of peace.

7. **Embrace Vulnerability:** True strength lies in vulnerability. Opening up to surrender builds deeper connections and an authentic sense of self.

8. **Focus on What You Can Control:** Surrender doesn't mean losing control over everything. Choose to act in areas you can influence, like your responses, attitudes, and actions.

9. **Practice Gratitude:** Let gratitude ground you in the present. Appreciate the lessons each step of surrender offers, allowing it to bring peace and perspective.

10. **Celebrate Small Wins:** Every choice to surrender, however minor, is a victory in self-discovery and growth.

As individuals embrace these principles, they navigate recovery with resilience, finding strength not just in overcoming challenges but in connecting more deeply with themselves and others.

In junior high, I worked part-time for a young man who had just started his own furniture upholstery business. We'd pick up worn-out furniture in his clunky old GM Suburban, haul it to his shop, and then deliver it back after it was expertly reupholstered. It was the only time in my life I drank Pepsi, cracking a can open after a long day pulling staples, prying out nails, and even tying springs. He was an unusual guy, humorous and offbeat—a mentor of sorts—and I admired his dedication and creativity. His young wife made the best broiled hamburgers I've ever had.

One day, he shared a story with me that would later become my personal definition of external validation. His ultimate vision of success was to buy a brand-new Cadillac, meticulously wash and wax it, and park it right outside Classic's Drug Store, the cornerstone of our little town in Woodland, Michigan. In his fantasy, he'd step out of his gleaming car, stretch, and casually comment on the heat of the day. Then, he'd walk around to the trunk, pull out an enormous axe, and—without any hesitation—hack off the car's roof. When he'd finished, he'd calmly put the roof and the axe in the trunk, get back in, and drive off as if nothing had happened.

This was my first introduction to the power and absurdity of external validation. He wanted to shock people, to make them look twice and wonder about his motives. That Cadillac, a symbol of status and success, wasn't enough. He needed others to see it, to be in awe of it, and to question his defiance of it. This story left an impression on me, teaching me early on about the pitfalls of needing validation from others. It's a lesson I've carried with me, reminding me to find validation within rather than searching for it in others' eyes.

One of the early and persistent challenges in sobriety groups, especially AA, has been the "God question." The AA model encourages spirituality, yet the language is often rooted in Christian terminology, leading some to feel isolated or pressured to adapt beliefs they may not hold. This has inspired secular alternatives, echoing the AA framework but offering a non-theistic approach to recovery, focusing instead on personal growth and community support.

The need for AA to remain neutral on religion and politics has always been emphasized. Yet, the foundational references to God—mainly from a Christian worldview—can feel exclusionary, unintentionally underscoring why Christian temperance movements spearheaded early advocacy for sobriety. Biblical stories, such as that of Noah becoming intoxicated after planting a vineyard, found in Genesis 9:20-21, have contributed to this association. The Bible is filled with such accounts, which played a role in fueling these movements and continue to echo in recovery dialogues today.

This religious thread reminds us that, while a sense of "higher power" can be transformative in recovery, it's essential for support networks to respect diverse beliefs, accommodating people from all walks of life. With more inclusive, non-religious language, recovery programs can foster unity, empathy, and shared healing regardless of individual spiritual paths.

AA's approach to spirituality, particularly through its references to "God as you understand Him," has led to both strength and division within the recovery community. While the traditional model has helped countless individuals, it undeniably aligns more closely with Christian values, which can leave non-Christian members feeling disconnected from the core language and philosophy. For those who do not seek divine intervention, it's reasonable to question why a "higher power" would suddenly intervene in their personal recovery. This ongoing disconnect has inspired the formation of secular alternatives, which embrace many of AA's structural benefits without relying on religious themes.

Secular recovery frameworks take an evidence-based approach, empowering individuals to regain control of their lives through science-driven, tangible practices. These include:

1. **Professional Help**: Engage with addiction specialists, therapists, or medical professionals who provide customized recovery plans.

2. **Support Groups**: Join secular groups like SMART Recovery or LifeRing, which offer non-religious, community-based support.

3. **Behavioral Therapy**: Use Cognitive Behavioral Therapy (CBT) to address underlying emotional triggers and equip oneself with practical coping mechanisms.

4. **Lifestyle Changes**: Foster health through improved nutrition, exercise, and stress management, all of which support long-term recovery.

5. **Education**: Educate oneself on the neurological effects of addiction to understand it as a medical condition rather than a moral failing.

6. **Goal Setting**: Set achievable, realistic goals that nurture personal motivation and accountability, which can be transformative in creating a structured recovery path.

These secular methods, grounded in rational and scientific practices, provide clear steps for navigating recovery while aligning with an individual's unique perspectives and needs. An essential principle within secular recovery is **non-attachment**, a concept that Buddhist teachings also explore extensively. In Buddhism, non-attachment is a way to reduce suffering by letting go of dependency on external circumstances and cultivating inner peace. Engaging with texts on non-attachment or practicing mindfulness and body awareness techniques, like body scans, can help identify and understand how attachments to various triggers manifest within one's body and mind.

This dual approach—drawing on secular, scientific practices alongside mindfulness principles—can create a balanced recovery path that empowers individuals to heal on their terms, free from the constraints of any one philosophy.

In our journey toward recovery and personal growth, recognizing the impermanent nature of life—and examining the things we cling to—can be transformative. This reflection helps us understand how our attachments, whether to objects, people, or outcomes, impact our emotions and well-being.

Exploring the concept of impermanence begins with reflecting on the transient nature of life, relationships, and personal goals. Spend time in nature, where the cycles of growth and decay serve as gentle reminders that everything changes. Writing about this can provide clarity, helping to bring awareness to the shifts within us and around us.

Consider making a list of attachments you hold tightly, noting specific objects, people, or outcomes you're invested in. Reflect on how each affects your emotions and sense of peace. Start small by choosing one attachment to release, like decluttering a space or setting boundaries in a challenging relationship. These small steps of letting go can foster a lighter, more mindful approach to daily life.

Keeping a gratitude journal helps redirect focus from what's lacking to what's present. Noticing and appreciating the richness of each moment can reduce longing and foster a sense of contentment. A practice of kindness without expectation also nurtures connection without attachment. When we help others selflessly, we foster a stronger sense of community and purpose.

Finally, take time to reassess the dynamics in your relationships. Healthy connections support growth, while others may lead to dependency or unhealthy attachment. Setting boundaries in these cases allows for personal growth, encouraging more balanced and supportive relationships.

These steps can help us engage with life's impermanence in a meaningful way. By learning to let go of certain attachments, we open ourselves to greater inner peace and a more mindful, fulfilling life.

Learning to communicate clearly within relationships is essential for expressing needs without fostering feelings of obligation. Cultivating non-attachment becomes easier in supportive environments, so joining a meditation group or a mindfulness-focused community can provide insight and reinforce these principles.

Working with a therapist familiar with non-attachment can also help identify and address deeply ingrained attachments, guiding you toward a mindset that embraces change. Setting aside time each month to reflect on progress can be enlightening: ask yourself, what attachments have you released? In what ways has your perspective shifted?

Adopt a flexible approach, adjusting your plans and practices as needed based on what resonates. Gradually integrate mindfulness into everyday actions, focusing on each task without becoming attached to the outcome. Set goals for personal growth, but let the journey itself become the point of fulfillment, rather than the destination. With this approach, we foster non-attachment, promoting both peace and purpose, while also reducing the hold that addictive behaviors may have over our lives.

The Agnostic Twelve Steps by Bill W

1. **Acknowledgment of Powerlessness:**

We admitted we were powerless over alcohol—that our lives had become unmanageable.

Recognizing the impact of our choices is the first step toward change. This acknowledgment is not a sign of defeat but a courageous admission of our struggles.

2. **Belief in Restoration:**

Came to believe that we could restore ourselves to sanity.

We cultivate the understanding that recovery is possible through our own efforts and support from others.

3. **Decision to Seek Understanding:**

Made a decision to turn our will and our lives over to the care of our understanding.

This step invites us to engage with our personal values and beliefs, guiding our journey toward healing.

4. **Fearless Self-Inventory:**

Made a searching and fearless moral inventory of ourselves.

Taking the time to reflect deeply on our actions and motivations allows us to understand our behavior and its effects on ourselves and others.

5. **Admission of Wrongs:**

Admitted to ourselves and to another human being the exact nature of our wrongs.

Sharing our truths with a trusted person fosters connection and accountability, helping to alleviate the burdens we carry.

6. Readiness for Change:

Were entirely ready to have our character defects removed.

This readiness is a pivotal moment, where we open ourselves to the possibility of transformation and growth.

7. Humbly Seeking Improvement:

Humbly ask ourselves to remove our shortcomings.

This step emphasizes the importance of self-awareness and the willingness to work on our flaws, creating space for positive change.

8. Willingness to Make Amends:

Made a list of all persons we had harmed and became willing to make amends to them all.

Identifying those we've hurt is crucial in our journey. It is a commitment to take responsibility for our actions and their impact on others.

9. Direct Amends:

Made direct amends to such people wherever possible, except when to do so would injure them or others.

Taking action to repair our relationships is an important step in healing, fostering forgiveness and understanding.

10. Ongoing Self-Reflection:

Continued to take personal inventory and when we were wrong promptly admitted it.

Regular self-assessment helps us remain accountable and aware, enabling continuous growth and learning from our experiences.

11. Reflection and Mindfulness:

Sought through reflection and mindfulness to improve our conscious contact with reality as we understood it.

Practicing mindfulness allows us to engage with our thoughts and feelings in a constructive way, grounding ourselves in the present moment.

12. Sharing the Journey:

Having had an awakening as a result of these steps, we tried to carry this message to others and practice these principles in all our affairs.

Our recovery journey is enriched when we share our experiences with others, offering support and encouragement while reinforcing our own commitment to these principles.

These steps, crafted by Bill W, provide a supportive framework for individuals seeking recovery, focusing on personal growth, accountability, and the importance of community without requiring belief in a higher power.

We believed it was our parental duty to expose our daughters to the church, an obligation that seemed to echo guilt from our own upbringing. In my quest to provide them with a sense of community, I found an unexpected avenue through my involvement in a men's city league basketball team. One of my teammates, an outstanding rebounder, happened to be a Presbyterian minister. It felt serendipitous—what better reason to start attending his church with my family than this connection?

From the moment we stepped into that new church, I felt a sense of belonging. The warmth of the congregation wrapped around us like a comforting blanket. Over time, we became members, drawn into the vibrant life of the church community.

As I delved deeper, I discovered that Presbyterians are a group of Christians with roots in Europe, who had formed a church based on a more representative style of governance. Fascinatingly, their principles even served as a template for the emerging democratic government of the United States. The realization that many of our founding fathers shared this faith, embodying a spirit of civil disobedience and progressive thought, captivated me. They had rejected outdated European norms surrounding church and politics, opting instead to forge a new path.

My newfound enthusiasm for the church flourished, and I became active in various activities, eventually serving on the Board of Trustees for several years. I was eager to contribute, feeling a deep sense of purpose in supporting a community that aligned with my values.

However, despite my engagement, I grappled with significant doubts. The concept of original sin weighed heavily on me, and many Bible stories, particularly those from the Old Testament, seemed too fantastical to accept. I wanted to believe, yet the reliance on alternate interpretations and questionable translations felt like a veil obscuring the truth. My inner conflict grew; the symbolism and metaphors didn't satisfy my quest for authenticity.

As time passed, I began to drift away from Christianity, feeling more like a retired Christian than an active participant in the faith. This departure was not an act of rebellion but rather a painful acknowledgment of my evolving beliefs. I struggled to reconcile my love for the community and the teachings that no longer resonated with my understanding of the world.

Reflecting on this journey, I recognize that faith is a deeply personal endeavor, and my path, though different, is valid. I still cherish the lessons learned within the church and the connections formed there. Each step, from my initial attendance to my eventual departure, shaped my understanding of community, belief, and personal growth.

Anyone who experiences a shift in their belief system deserves respect and a non-judgmental atmosphere. I strive to ensure that this respect flows both ways, fostering an environment where open dialogue can thrive. This understanding is at the core of my approach to recovery: a journey that is spiritual rather than strictly religious.

Living a loving and compassionate life today feels infinitely more rewarding than the alternative of cashing in my insurance policy. The thought of embracing life, even amidst uncertainty, fuels my desire to nurture not only my own growth but also the growth of those around me. So, while I wait for the afterlife chips to fall as they may, I find solace in simple pleasures—like fertilizing the lilac bush in my backyard. Nature grounds me, reminding me of the beauty and transience of life. I've never reacted well to threats; perhaps that's the alcoholic in me, seeking comfort in familiar routines rather than facing fears head-on.

About five or six years ago, I began an enlightening journey into ancient literature, exploring works that predate the birth of Christ by several centuries—even reaching back thousands of years. The intellect of these ancient minds continues to astonish me. For instance, *The* Epic of Gilgamesh delves into themes of excess and the quest for immortality. Its reflections resonate deeply within me, shedding light on the timeless human struggles that mirror our contemporary battles with addiction and recovery.

Through this exploration, I've learned that the essence of our struggles—be it in faith, addiction, or the pursuit of meaning—is rooted in our shared humanity. The narratives from ancient texts remind us that we are not alone in our challenges; we are part of a continuum of seekers striving for understanding and connection.

As I share these reflections, I hope to cultivate empathy and connection with others who may be on their own journeys. Each story, whether from an ancient civilization or our modern lives, holds the potential to inspire, heal, and unite us in our quest for a meaningful existence. In this way, I find strength in community, knowing that we can support one another as we navigate the complexities of life, faith, and recovery.

Gilgamesh's journey serves as a powerful reminder that seeking fulfillment through hedonism is ultimately unfulfilling. His story reflects a profound message about the importance of moderation and self-awareness. In our modern lives, this ancient wisdom resonates strongly, particularly as we navigate the complexities of addiction and recovery.

Similarly, the Rigveda, the foundational text for Hinduism, contains hymns that emphasize the significance of moderation and self-control, especially concerning the use of intoxicants. While some verses celebrate the use of Soma, a ritual drink, others caution against excess, promoting a balanced and disciplined life. This duality reflects a broader message that values sobriety and mindfulness. In our fast-paced world, where the allure of indulgence often overshadows the benefits of restraint, the Rigveda's teachings encourage us to pause, reflect, and prioritize our well-being.

Reggae Vida, one of the oldest sacred texts of Hinduism, weaves a rich tapestry of hymns that explore various aspects of life, spirituality, and the human experience. Although it doesn't explicitly address alcoholism as a modern issue, its teachings provide invaluable insights into the nature of addiction, emphasizing the importance of self-control and the pursuit of a balanced life. The Rigveda suggests that deviations from this balance, such as alcoholism, disrupt not only physical health but also mental and spiritual well-being.

By examining these ancient themes, we can glean a holistic approach to treating alcoholism that aligns with the spiritual and philosophical foundations of the Rigveda. It highlights how addiction is a deviation from the natural order and spiritual harmony. The text emphasizes living in accordance with Dharma—righteousness—and maintaining balance in our lives. Alcoholism, as a disruption of this balance, can lead to profound suffering.

As we reflect on our actions and the consequences they bring, the Rigveda promotes self-awareness as a crucial step toward recovery. This self-awareness fosters the understanding that acknowledging our struggles is not a sign of weakness but a vital aspect of personal growth. It reminds us that we are not alone on this journey; we have the capacity to learn from the past and strive for a more balanced existence.

In sharing these insights, I hope to cultivate empathy and connection among those who may be navigating their own paths to recovery. Each step taken toward understanding ourselves better, whether through ancient wisdom or personal experience, is a testament to our resilience and a commitment to living a fulfilling life.

Connecting with spiritual practices such as prayer, meditation, and rituals can provide individuals with the strength and motivation necessary to combat addiction. These practices foster a deeper understanding of ourselves, encouraging self-reflection and mindfulness. Furthermore, the sense of community created through shared rituals and gatherings builds a vital support network for those grappling with alcohol dependence. It's within this collective embrace that individuals often find the encouragement needed to face their challenges head-on.

In ancient literature, themes of moderation and the consequences of excess are poignantly illustrated in *The Iliad* and *The Odyssey*. While these epic narratives celebrate moments of drinking and revelry, they also serve as cautionary tales, highlighting the dangers of hubris and the critical importance of self-control. Characters who indulge excessively often face dire consequences, reinforcing the need for sobriety and discipline.

The Iliad and *The Odyssey*, attributed to Homer, delve into profound themes such as honor, heroism, and the human condition. Among these themes, the treatment of alcohol and its effects on characters offers a nuanced commentary on its role in society. In *The Iliad*, alcohol frequently appears in scenes of feasting and celebration, intricately woven into the fabric of warrior culture. The consumption of wine acts as a means of camaraderie and bonding among warriors, yet it also serves as a catalyst for conflict. The infamous quarrel between Achilles and Agamemnon, for instance, is exacerbated by tensions surrounding pride and honor, heightened within the context of drinking.

Reflecting on these narratives, we can draw parallels to our contemporary struggles with addiction. The excesses depicted in these epics remind us that the pursuit of fulfillment through indulgence can lead to turmoil and chaos. Just as the characters in these stories grapple with their flaws, we too must confront the aspects of ourselves that seek escape through substances.

By engaging with these ancient themes, we cultivate a holistic approach to treating alcoholism, rooted in the spiritual and philosophical insights of the past. The emphasis on moderation and self-awareness resonates deeply with our modern experience. Recognizing that addiction can disrupt our balance and lead to physical, mental, and spiritual suffering encourages us to reflect on our actions and their consequences.

Ultimately, the wisdom found in these texts emphasizes the importance of living in accordance with our values and maintaining harmony in our lives. Alcoholism disrupts this balance, but by fostering self-awareness and community support, we can navigate the path to recovery with greater resilience. In sharing these insights, I hope to inspire readers to reflect on their own journeys, drawing strength from both ancient wisdom and modern practices. Together, we can embrace sobriety as a collective effort, nurturing each other toward a healthier, more fulfilling life.

Alcohol symbolizes both the joys of fellowship and the potential for destructive behavior. It enhances social bonds but can also lead to strife and discord. This duality is vividly portrayed in *The Odyssey*, particularly through the character of Odysseus. His encounters with various cultures illustrate the multifaceted nature of wine. For instance, in the land of the Cyclopes, Odysseus cleverly uses wine to intoxicate Polyphemus, showcasing alcohol as a tool for cunning and survival in a perilous world.

This complexity is not limited to Homer's works; it resonates deeply within the *Hebrew Bible*, also known as the *Tanakh*. Here, the text acknowledges the cultural significance of wine while presenting a nuanced message about moderation and responsibility. Throughout the *Hebrew Bible*, wine is often depicted as a source of joy and blessing. For instance, in Psalms, wine is described as something that "gladdens the heart of man." This acknowledgment of wine as a gift is accompanied by caution, reminding us that while it can enhance our lives, it can also lead to peril if consumed without awareness.

Reflecting on these literary themes, we can see how they apply to our modern struggles with addiction. The narratives of *The Iliad* and *The Odyssey* serve as reminders that indulgence can have serious consequences, emphasizing the importance of self-control. Just as the characters face challenges tied to their consumption of alcohol, we too must confront our relationship with substances and recognize the impact they have on our lives.

By examining these texts, we glean valuable insights into the nature of addiction and the importance of balance. The struggles depicted in ancient literature resonate with our contemporary battles, encouraging us to cultivate self-awareness and moderation. As we navigate our recovery journeys, these lessons remind us that we are not alone; we share a long history of seeking understanding and balance.

In embracing these teachings, we create a supportive environment where individuals can reflect on their actions and their consequences. This self-awareness is not merely an intellectual exercise but a crucial step toward recovery. Recognizing the potential dangers of excess can empower us to make conscious choices, fostering a healthier relationship with ourselves and our communities.

Ultimately, the lessons found in *The Odyssey*, the *Hebrew Bible*, and other ancient texts highlight the dual nature of alcohol and its role in our lives. By acknowledging both its joys and risks, we can approach sobriety with a holistic mindset, promoting mindfulness and balance as we support one another on this shared journey. Together, we can celebrate the triumphs of fellowship while remaining vigilant against the pitfalls of excess, fostering a community grounded in compassion, understanding, and resilience.

Alcohol symbolizes both the joys of fellowship and the potential for destructive behavior. It can enhance social bonds, particularly during celebrations of religious festivals like Passover, where the ritual consumption of wine signifies joy and communal togetherness. This positive portrayal underscores wine's importance in ancient Israelite culture, reflecting a deep-rooted tradition of shared experiences.

Yet, the *Hebrew Bible* offers a cautionary perspective, warning against the pitfalls of excessive drinking. Proverbs states, "Wine is a mocker, strong drink is raging; and whosoever is deceived thereby is not wise." This verse highlights the duality of alcohol, suggesting that while it can be enjoyed in moderation, it may also lead to foolishness and moral degradation when abused.

The narrative of Noah serves as a poignant example. After becoming intoxicated, Noah's vulnerability exposes him to shame and conflict within his family, illustrating the potential consequences of overindulgence. This story resonates with anyone who has faced the repercussions of their choices, serving as a stark reminder that alcohol can blur our judgment and lead to destructive behaviors.

Moreover, the text often associates alcohol with negative behaviors and social issues. In Proverbs, the writer vividly describes the woes of a drunkard, highlighting how excessive drinking leads to strife, sorrow, and a lack of clarity. This passage serves as a compelling reminder of the destructive potential of alcoholism, emphasizing the need for self-control and the dangers of succumbing to temptation.

Reflecting on these themes, we can draw valuable lessons for our modern journeys toward recovery. Just as the characters in these ancient narratives grapple with the complexities of alcohol, we too must confront our relationships with substances. Understanding that alcohol can bring both joy and peril allows us to approach sobriety with a nuanced perspective.

As we navigate our paths to recovery, it is crucial to recognize that the lessons of moderation and self-awareness are timeless. These teachings remind us that we can enjoy life's pleasures while maintaining balance and responsibility. By fostering a supportive community where we share our struggles and triumphs, we create an environment that encourages growth and healing.

In sharing these reflections, I hope to inspire readers to engage with their own journeys, recognizing the dual nature of alcohol in their lives. Together, we can celebrate the moments of connection it brings while remaining vigilant about its potential pitfalls. Embracing this balance can empower us to build a healthier, more fulfilling relationship with ourselves and with each other.

The *Hebrew Bible* addresses the responsibilities of leaders regarding alcohol consumption. In Leviticus, priests are commanded not to consume wine or strong drink when entering the sanctuary. This directive underscores the importance of clarity of mind and moral integrity for those in positions of authority. It reminds us that leaders must set an example of moderation for the community, reinforcing the idea that alcohol can impair judgment and affect decision-making.

In conclusion, the *Hebrew Bible* presents a balanced view of alcohol, acknowledging its role in joy and celebration while simultaneously warning against the dangers of excess. Throughout various narratives and proverbs, it advocates for moderation and self-control, emphasizing the significance of responsible drinking. This duality invites us to celebrate the communal aspects of alcohol while recognizing its potential pitfalls.

For instance, the celebrations during religious festivals, such as Passover, highlight wine's positive role in fostering communal togetherness. Yet, wisdom literature warns us to remain vigilant against the excesses that can lead to foolishness and moral degradation. Proverbs vividly captures this sentiment, stating, "Wine is a mocker, strong drink is raging; and whosoever is deceived thereby is not wise."

The narrative of Noah serves as a poignant example. After becoming intoxicated, Noah's vulnerability exposes him to shame and conflict within his family, illustrating the far-reaching consequences of overindulgence. Moreover, the text often associates alcohol with negative behaviors and social issues. The writer of Proverbs describes the woes of a drunkard, emphasizing that excessive drinking can lead to strife, sorrow, and a lack of clarity.

These narratives resonate deeply with our contemporary struggles surrounding alcohol. They remind us that while we can enjoy the communal joys that alcohol may bring, we must approach it with caution and self-awareness. Just as Noah's story reflects the potential fallout of poor choices, we too must consider how our relationship with alcohol can impact our lives and those around us.

By engaging with these themes, we encourage a thoughtful examination of alcohol's place in our lives. We can learn to celebrate responsibly, fostering an environment of support and understanding within our communities.

As we navigate our journeys toward recovery, we must embrace the wisdom of moderation and self-control found within these ancient texts. By doing so, we can cultivate a healthier relationship with alcohol, honoring both its potential for joy and the necessity of responsible consumption. Together, we can foster a culture of awareness and support, encouraging one another to remain vigilant against the temptations of excess.

The *Tao Te Ching* promotes a philosophy of moderation, simplicity, and balance, serving as a profound form of sobriety. It encourages us to live in harmony with the Tao (the way) while avoiding excess and extremes. This ancient text advocates for self-restraint and mindfulness, suggesting that true wisdom arises from a balanced approach to life. In the context of alcoholism, the *Tao Te Ching* offers a path toward equilibrium.

Attributed to Laozi, the *Tao Te Ching* provides insights into existence, the importance of harmony, and the pursuit of balance. While it does not explicitly address alcoholism, its teachings offer a framework for understanding addiction and the journey toward sobriety through the lens of Taoist philosophy. Central to this philosophy are the principles of Yin and Yang, emphasizing the need for harmony within oneself and with the world.

Alcoholism often stems from an imbalance—whether emotional, psychological, or social. The *Tao Te Ching* encourages individuals to seek equilibrium in their lives, reminding us that acknowledging our need for balance can empower us to confront our addiction. This journey starts with recognizing that our desires, when left unchecked, can lead us astray.

The concept of *Wu Wei*, or the art of non-action, champions a return to simplicity and a rejection of excessive desires. Many individuals turn to alcohol in search of escape or pleasure, but the *Tao Te Ching* teaches us that true contentment lies not in external substances but in appreciating the simple joys of life. This idea resonates deeply with those in recovery, urging them to find fulfillment in authentic experiences rather than fleeting indulgences.

As we reflect on the teachings of the *Tao Te Ching*, we uncover valuable lessons applicable to our struggles with addiction. By embracing moderation and self-awareness, we can cultivate a healthier relationship with ourselves and our communities. The journey toward sobriety is not solely about abstaining from alcohol; it's about finding balance and harmony within ourselves.

In this process, the support of a community becomes essential. Just as the *Tao Te Ching* emphasizes the interconnectedness of all things, we too must recognize that recovery is often best pursued collectively. Sharing our experiences, challenges, and victories can create a powerful network of support, fostering resilience and understanding among individuals facing similar struggles.

By weaving the wisdom of the *Tao Te Ching* into our recovery narratives, we create a space for reflection and growth. Together, we can navigate the complexities of addiction, embracing the path to balance and moderation while encouraging one another along the way. This shared journey not only empowers us as individuals but also strengthens our collective resolve to live fulfilling, sober lives.

By embracing simplicity, individuals can rediscover fulfillment without the need for alcohol, cultivating a deeper connection with themselves and their surroundings. Practicing balance, simplicity, and compassion allows individuals to navigate their recovery journey with a sense of purpose and clarity. The principles of Taoism inspire a holistic approach to sobriety, emphasizing that true fulfillment comes from within and fostering a life aligned with one's authentic self. Through this search for balance, the path to recovery can transform into a profound journey of self-discovery and harmony.

Similarly, the Bhagavad Gita imparts timeless wisdom that teaches sobriety through concepts like self-control, moderation, and detachment. It emphasizes yoga as a discipline for achieving balance in life, advocating for moderation in eating, sleeping, and activities. The Gita encourages maintaining equanimity in pleasure and pain, success and failure, highlighting that true wisdom and fulfillment arise from a disciplined and sober mind focused on duty (*Dharma*) and spiritual growth.

In the Gita, we learn that life's challenges can be met with a calm and composed mindset. This perspective invites us to reflect on our own journeys, encouraging us to approach recovery with the understanding that every struggle can lead to greater self-awareness and growth. The teachings promote the idea that balance is not merely the absence of excess, but rather a harmonious alignment of our thoughts, actions, and intentions.

As we weave these ancient philosophies into our narratives of recovery, we foster a deeper connection with the core messages of moderation and mindfulness. Recognizing that alcoholism often arises from an imbalance—whether emotional, psychological, or social—empowers us to confront our struggles. The *Tao Te Ching* teaches that acknowledging this need for balance can motivate us to make conscious choices that resonate with our true selves.

Moreover, the *Bhagavad Gita* reminds us of the importance of self-discipline and commitment to personal growth. By embracing moderation, we not only honor ourselves but also set an example for others in our communities. As we cultivate self-awareness and compassion, we create a ripple effect that encourages those around us to engage thoughtfully with their own relationships to alcohol and other substances.

By integrating the wisdom of the *Tao Te Ching* and the *Bhagavad Gita* into our lives, we illuminate a path toward recovery that is enriched by the lessons of the past. Together, we can celebrate the journey toward sobriety, embracing both the challenges and triumphs that come with it. Through shared experiences, we build a supportive community that uplifts each other, reinforcing the idea that recovery is a team sport.

As we continue to navigate this journey, let us remain grounded in the teachings that emphasize the value of balance, mindfulness, and compassion. By doing so, we pave the way for a fulfilling life, one that reflects our authentic selves and honors the connections we share with others.

Siddhartha, the birth name of Gautama Buddha, embodies the transformative journey toward understanding the nature of suffering and the path to liberation. As a prince who renounced his privileged life, he wandered the Earth in search of deeper truths, ultimately attaining Enlightenment under the Bodhi tree in Bodh Gaya, India. This journey, though ancient, offers profound insights relevant to our contemporary struggles with addiction.

Buddha's teachings, known as the *Dharma*, emphasize the importance of self-awareness and moderation. While he does not explicitly address alcohol, his principles resonate deeply within the context of sobriety. The Four Noble Truths and the Eightfold Path serve as guiding principles for achieving liberation from suffering. In essence, the path to recovery mirrors the Buddha's quest for balance and clarity, teaching us that true fulfillment arises from within.

Similarly, the *Bhagavad Gita* imparts wisdom on self-control, moderation, and detachment. It emphasizes the practice of yoga as a discipline for achieving balance in life, advocating for moderation in eating, sleeping, and activities. The Gita teaches us to maintain equanimity in pleasure and pain, success and failure, highlighting that true wisdom and fulfillment come from a disciplined and sober mind focused on duty (*Dharma*) and spiritual growth.

Both the teachings of Siddhartha and the messages from the Gita encourage us to embrace simplicity and cultivate mindfulness. By doing so, individuals can rediscover fulfillment without reliance on alcohol, nurturing a deeper connection with themselves and the world around them. This journey fosters an environment where recovery becomes a path of self-discovery and harmony.

In embracing these ancient teachings, we find the courage to confront our struggles with addiction. Alcoholism often arises from an imbalance—be it emotional, psychological, or social. Recognizing this can motivate individuals to seek equilibrium in their lives, prompting conscious choices that align with their true selves. The practice of *Wu Wei,* or effortless action, encourages a rejection of excessive desires, inviting us to appreciate the simple joys of life instead of seeking escape through substances.

By weaving the wisdom of the *Tao Te Ching,* the insights of Siddhartha, and the teachings of the *Bhagavad Gita* into our narratives of recovery, we create a rich tapestry of understanding. Together, we can navigate the complexities of addiction, drawing strength from the ancient philosophies that advocate for balance, mindfulness, and compassion.

As we embark on this journey, let us remember that sobriety is not merely about abstaining from substances; it is about cultivating a life that resonates with our authentic selves. Through shared experiences and community support, we can inspire one another, fostering a culture of recovery rooted in understanding, resilience, and mutual respect. In this way, the journey toward sobriety transforms into a profound exploration of self-discovery, guiding us toward a life of harmony and fulfillment.

Gilgamesh is a legendary figure in ancient Mesopotamian mythology and literature, and his story offers profound insights into the human experience, particularly regarding the complexities of alcohol. As the main character in the *Epic of Gilgamesh,* one of the earliest known recorded works of literature, he embodies the struggles of power, friendship, and the quest for immortality. Historically, Gilgamesh was a king of the Sumerian city-state of Uruk, and his tale intertwines mythology with the values and beliefs of the Sumerian and Akkadian civilizations.

In the epic, Gilgamesh is portrayed as a powerful and arrogant king who embarks on a quest for immortality following the death of his beloved friend, Enkidu. This journey serves as a poignant backdrop for exploring the themes of friendship, mortality, and the search for meaning in life. One notable episode involves Enkidu, who transitions from a wild man living among animals to a more human-like figure through his introduction to civilization. This transformation is catalyzed by his encounter with a woman named Shamhat, who tempts him with food and beer, symbolizing the shift from a primal existence to a more cultured life.

This introduction to alcohol reflects both its allure and its potential dangers. Enkidu's experiences with beer highlight the dual nature of alcohol as a source of pleasure and a catalyst for change. While it brings him into a new world, it also signifies the loss of his original wildness, suggesting that indulgence can lead to both positive and negative consequences.

The *Epic of Gilgamesh* includes scenes of feasting and drinking that emphasize the social and cultural importance of alcohol in ancient Mesopotamian society. However, the narrative also underscores the necessity of balance, illustrating how excess can lead to loss of control. The interactions among the characters often reveal the darker side of indulgence, reinforcing the idea that moderation is key to maintaining one's integrity and well-being.

The depth of thought captured in this ancient work is striking, particularly when we consider the examples of addictive behavior depicted thousands of years ago. The *Epic of Gilgamesh* serves as a reminder that the challenges we face today are not new; they are part of a longstanding human struggle. Just as Gilgamesh and Enkidu grappled with the implications of their choices, we too must confront our relationships with substances and the impacts they have on our lives and communities.

By reflecting on these themes, we can draw valuable lessons for our own journeys toward recovery. The wisdom embedded in the *Epic of Gilgamesh* encourages us to navigate the complexities of addiction with a deeper understanding of our motivations and the consequences of our actions. As we strive for balance in our lives, we can honor the transformative potential of our experiences, finding strength in the bonds we create with ourselves and with others.

Ultimately, the story of Gilgamesh inspires us to engage thoughtfully with our struggles and triumphs, reminding us that the path to recovery is a journey of self-discovery. By sharing these ancient insights, we foster a sense of community and resilience that can guide us through the challenges of addiction, illuminating our path toward a more fulfilling and harmonious life.

CHAPTER TEN

THE ATHLETIC CONFERENCE: PUBLIC OR PAROCHIAL

THROUGHOUT MY EXPLORATION OF ANCIENT RELIGIONS, I have been surprised by the striking similarities in their teachings regarding right and wrong, the dos and don'ts that predate even the Ten Commandments. This realization has guided my own path, particularly through my introduction to Buddhism. In Buddhism, the concept of a higher power is optional, allowing for compatibility with other spiritual traditions.

My intent with this book on sobriety is not to convert anyone to a specific belief system. Rather, I aim to ensure that neither religion nor a lack of it serves as a barrier on the path to recovery. I have witnessed far too many scared and fragile newcomers who let the notion of religion deter them from attending AA meetings. It is disheartening to think that such fears could keep someone from the support and healing that recovery offers.

Spirituality should not be co-opted by religion. Mindfulness and meditation should not be confined to spiritual practices alone. I observe that the "God" concept has caused many fragile individuals to shy away from Alcoholics Anonymous and similar group teachings. It is vital to recognize that alcoholics need assistance from sources beyond themselves. For those who are Christian, it is only logical that their God could be a source of guidance. This idea seems simple enough and, in my view, it should be embraced.

In Buddhism, belief in a higher power is not a prerequisite for personal growth. Instead, mindfulness, meditation, and other mental health strategies reflect each individual's unique journey. This inclusivity allows for a broader interpretation of recovery, inviting people from various backgrounds to explore what sobriety means for them without fear of judgment or exclusion.

The journey to sobriety is profoundly personal, and it is my hope that readers find pathways that resonate with their experiences, regardless of their spiritual beliefs. The principles of mindfulness and self-reflection can be transformative, offering tools that foster resilience and promote healing. Embracing a community where individuals feel safe to share their struggles, devoid of religious constraints, can cultivate an environment of compassion and understanding.

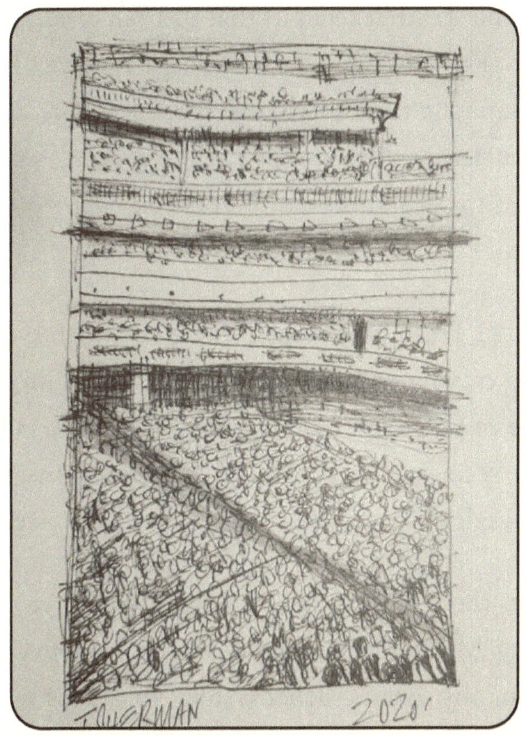

As we navigate the challenges of addiction, let us celebrate the diversity of beliefs that contribute to our shared humanity. Recovery is a team sport, and it thrives in a space that honors individual journeys while fostering collective support. By opening our hearts and minds to various perspectives, we can create a welcoming community that guides everyone toward a brighter, sober future.

At the heart of Buddhism lies the Four Noble Truths, foundational teachings that offer profound insights into the nature of suffering and the journey toward liberation. The first Noble Truth, *dukkha*, reminds us that suffering is an inherent part of existence. This suffering manifests in various forms, from physical and emotional pain to the underlying dissatisfaction that often colors the human experience.

The second Noble Truth teaches us that the root of suffering is craving or attachment. These desires can take shape in many forms—greed, longing, or clinging to the impermanent aspects of life. Understanding this truth is crucial for those on the path to sobriety, as it reveals how our attachment to substances can perpetuate cycles of suffering and dissatisfaction.

The third Noble Truth offers hope: there is a way to end suffering. By eliminating craving and attachment, one can attain liberation and achieve a state of peace and contentment. This idea is liberating for individuals in recovery, suggesting that freedom from addiction is attainable through self-awareness and conscious choice.

As I reflect on these teachings, I am reminded of my own journey toward sobriety. My aim in sharing this book is not to convert anyone to Buddhism or any specific belief system. Instead, I want to create a space where spirituality is accessible to all, free from the constraints of dogma or fear. I've encountered many fragile newcomers who shy away from support groups like Alcoholics Anonymous due to apprehensions about religious expectations. It pains me to see how these fears can deter someone from the healing process.

Spirituality should not be co-opted by religion. The practices of mindfulness and meditation can be powerful tools for anyone seeking recovery, regardless of their religious beliefs. In Buddhism, the notion of a higher power is optional, allowing individuals to explore their personal paths without the pressure of traditional religious frameworks.

The journey toward sobriety is deeply personal, and I believe it should be inclusive and supportive. By emphasizing principles like mindfulness and meditation, we can foster an environment where individuals feel safe to explore their own spirituality or lack thereof, without judgment. Recovery is a collaborative effort, and we must create communities that welcome diverse perspectives and experiences.

As we navigate the complexities of addiction, let us draw strength from the teachings of Buddhism and the universal truths they contain. These teachings encourage us to confront our struggles with compassion and understanding, highlighting that the path to recovery can be a journey of self-discovery. By embracing these principles, we empower ourselves and others to pursue a fulfilling, sober life rooted in balance and mindfulness.

Together, we can build a supportive community that uplifts and inspires, reminding each other that sobriety is not just a personal endeavor but a collective journey toward healing and growth.

The *Fourth Noble Truth* outlines the *Eightfold Path*, which serves as a roadmap to the cessation of suffering and the achievement of enlightenment. This path offers practical guidance that can be particularly valuable for those on a journey toward sobriety. Here's a closer look at each aspect of the Eightfold Path and how it can apply to our lives:

1. **Right Understanding**: This involves developing a clear comprehension of the Four Noble Truths and the nature of reality. For individuals in recovery, this means acknowledging the reality of their addiction and understanding how it impacts their lives and relationships. By cultivating this understanding, we can begin to see the path forward.

2. **Right Intention**: This entails fostering thoughts and intentions rooted in renunciation, goodwill, and harmlessness. In the context of sobriety, it means setting a sincere intention to overcome addiction, nurturing compassion for oneself and others, and committing to a life that seeks to do no harm.

3. **Right Speech**: Speaking truthfully, kindly, and meaningfully is essential for building healthy relationships. For those in recovery, right speech involves communicating openly about struggles, offering support to fellow travelers on this path, and avoiding harmful language that can perpetuate shame or guilt.

4. **Right Action**: Acting ethically and non-harmfully according to Buddhist principles is crucial. This principle encourages individuals to engage in behaviors that promote well-being, both for themselves and for those around them, fostering a supportive environment essential for recovery.

5. **Right Livelihood**: Engaging in a livelihood that does not harm others aligns with Buddhist values and contributes to personal integrity. For individuals in recovery, this might mean seeking work that supports their new lifestyle, reinforcing their commitment to sobriety while nurturing a sense of purpose.

6. **Right Effort**: Making continuous efforts to cultivate positive qualities and eliminate negative ones is vital for personal growth. In recovery, this means actively working to replace harmful habits with constructive practices that promote well-being and resilience.

7. **Right Mindfulness**: Developing an awareness of one's body, feelings, mind, and phenomena can help individuals become more attuned to their experiences. Practicing mindfulness encourages a deeper understanding of cravings and triggers, empowering individuals to respond thoughtfully rather than react impulsively.

8. **Right Concentration**: Cultivating mental focus through meditation is a powerful tool for developing a deep state of concentration. For those on the path of recovery, meditation can serve as a means to quiet the mind, fostering clarity and insight that support a sober lifestyle.

By embracing the *Eightfold Path*, individuals can navigate their recovery journey with purpose and clarity. Each step encourages us to reflect on our actions and intentions, reinforcing the idea that sobriety is not merely the absence of alcohol but a holistic approach to living a balanced life.

These teachings from Buddhism provide a framework for understanding addiction and the journey toward sobriety. As we explore these concepts, let's remember that the path to recovery is deeply personal and can be enriched by mindfulness, compassion, and the support of a community. By incorporating the principles of the Eightfold Path into our lives, we can foster a deeper connection with ourselves and others, ultimately leading us to a place of healing and enlightenment.

By following the Eightfold Path, Buddhists aim to attain liberation from suffering and ultimately reach a state of Nirvana. This path offers practical guidance that resonates deeply with those seeking recovery from addiction.

While *Alcoholics Anonymous (AA)* traditionally emphasizes a higher power in a religious context, this concept can be reinterpreted through a more secular or Buddhist lens. Surrendering to the interconnectedness of all beings or to the wisdom of the universe allows individuals to find strength in their shared humanity. Instead of viewing a higher power solely as a deity, one can see it as the inherent Buddha nature within themselves—a recognition that we all possess the capacity for compassion, growth, and healing.

Turning one's will and life over to this understanding can cultivate humility and acceptance. It reminds us that our actions have consequences and that the ego often seeks to control outcomes, which can lead to suffering. By acknowledging this, we open ourselves to the transformative power of vulnerability.

Taking a moral inventory, a crucial step in recovery, aligns well with the Buddhist practices of self-reflection and mindfulness. By honestly examining our thoughts, actions, and intentions, we gain insight into the underlying causes of our addiction. This self-examination is not merely a checklist but a compassionate exploration of our true selves.

Admitting our wrongs to a higher power, ourselves, and another person involves a profound act of self-awareness and honesty. In a Buddhist context, this acknowledgment fosters personal growth and transformation, illuminating the path forward. It may take time to fully embrace this process, but remember: there is no rush in recovery. Each step is an opportunity for deeper understanding.

Being entirely ready to have a higher power remove our character defects signifies a willingness to let go of harmful patterns of behavior and thought. It represents an active commitment to positive change, embodying the Buddhist principle of *non-attachment*. By cultivating this openness, we allow ourselves to transform old habits into new practices that align with our authentic selves.

Humbly asking a higher power to remove our shortcomings reflects a fundamental Buddhist principle: the importance of seeking guidance and support from sources of wisdom and compassion, whether that wisdom comes from within ourselves or an external source. This humility is not just an acknowledgment of our limitations; it's an open invitation for transformation, allowing us to shed the burdens of our past and embrace a path toward healing.

Making a list of persons harmed and being willing to make amends signifies more than just a step in recovery; it's an act of deep reflection on the impact of our actions. In the Buddhist context, this step emphasizes the interconnectedness of all beings and the vital role of cultivating compassion and empathy. By recognizing how our choices affect others, we not only foster forgiveness but also begin to heal the wounds we've inflicted—on ourselves and those around us.

Making direct amends to such people whenever possible, except when to do so would cause harm, involves taking concrete actions to repair the damage done. This step is about accountability, a crucial aspect of growth. It requires courage to face those we've hurt and to take responsibility for our actions. Through this process, we learn that true strength lies not in evading our mistakes but in confronting them head-on, allowing us to transform pain into a powerful catalyst for change.

In Buddhism, the practice of making amends aligns seamlessly with the principles of right speech, right action, and compassion. This journey toward healing emphasizes that acknowledging our past actions is a crucial step in fostering both personal growth and the well-being of others.

Continuing to take personal inventory and promptly admitting when wrong reinforces the importance of ongoing self-reflection and accountability. This practice, essential in both Buddhism and addiction recovery, invites individuals to engage in an honest dialogue with themselves. It encourages a deeper understanding of how their actions resonate with their values and affect those around them, fostering a sense of humility and openness to change.

Seeking through prayer and meditation to improve conscious contact with a higher power can be interpreted as cultivating mindfulness and spiritual practices. These practices deepen one's connection with the present moment, allowing for a more profound experience of compassion and wisdom within oneself. This step invites individuals to explore their inner landscape, recognizing that true strength often arises from vulnerability and acceptance.

Sharing one's experiences, strength, and hope with others struggling with addiction embodies the essence of community and support. By living the principles of the Twelve Steps in a Buddhist context, individuals can align their recovery journey with the practices of compassion, generosity, and selflessness. This commitment to helping others find freedom from suffering creates a powerful ripple effect, nurturing a sense of connection and shared purpose among those on the path to sobriety.

Incorporating Buddhist principles into the interpretation of the Twelve Steps can provide individuals in recovery with valuable tools and perspectives to support their journey toward healing and transformation. By blending the wisdom of both traditions, individuals can deepen their self-understanding and cultivate mindfulness and compassion, which are essential for navigating the challenges of recovery.

Mindfulness allows individuals to stay present with their thoughts and emotions, fostering awareness of their actions and their impact on others. This practice encourages individuals to observe their experiences without judgment, promoting a healthier relationship with their feelings and urges.

Compassion, a core tenet of Buddhism, can significantly enhance the recovery process. By nurturing thoughts of compassion and non-harm, individuals can extend kindness toward themselves and others, creating an environment conducive to healing. This compassionate approach softens the harshness of self-criticism and allows for growth through understanding rather than shame.

Right Speech emphasizes the importance of speaking truthfully and kindly, avoiding harmful words that can inflict pain. In the context of recovery, this principle encourages open and honest communication, fostering trust within support networks and enabling deeper connections with others who share similar struggles.

Right Action calls for ethical behavior that aligns with the principles of kindness and non-harm. For those in recovery, this translates into making choices that promote personal well-being and the well-being of others. By actively choosing actions that reflect compassion, individuals not only enhance their recovery journey but also contribute positively to their communities.

By integrating these Buddhist principles into their recovery, individuals can cultivate a holistic approach that nurtures both their spirit and their capacity for transformation. This synergy between the Twelve Steps and Buddhist teachings can create a profound path toward lasting change and fulfillment.

The concept of **Right Livelihood** emphasizes engaging in work that does not harm others, aligning seamlessly with the principles of Alcoholics Anonymous (AA) and rooted in Christian spirituality. The Twelve Steps are thoughtfully designed to be applicable to individuals from various religious backgrounds or even those who identify as non-religious. This inclusivity fosters a welcoming environment for all seeking recovery.

Buddhism, with its focus on mindfulness, compassion, and self-awareness, offers profound insights when examining the Twelve Steps through a Buddhist lens. By recognizing the importance of these principles, individuals can enrich their recovery journey.

Admitting Powerlessness over alcohol or addiction resonates with the Buddhist acknowledgment of the impermanence and unsatisfactoriness of worldly desires and attachments. This crucial step lays the foundation for liberation from suffering, as it encourages individuals to confront their vulnerabilities honestly.

Recognizing one's inability to control addiction aligns with the Buddhist practice of letting go of attachments. This process encourages individuals to embrace the concept of impermanence and acknowledge their limitations.

The principle of **Right Effort** involves cultivating wholesome qualities while actively working to overcome unwholesome tendencies. This commitment to personal growth parallels the journey of recovery, where individuals strive to replace harmful habits with positive actions.

Right Mindfulness encourages an awareness of one's thoughts, feelings, and surroundings, which is essential in recovery. By practicing mindfulness, individuals can observe their cravings and emotional responses without judgment, allowing for healthier coping mechanisms.

Right Concentration, achieved through practices such as meditation, fosters a focused and clear mind, essential for navigating the complexities of recovery. Meditation serves as a powerful tool for self-reflection, helping individuals gain insight into their behaviors and motivations.

By following the Eightfold Path, Buddhists seek to develop wisdom, ethical conduct, and mental discipline, ultimately leading to the cessation of suffering and the attainment of enlightenment or Nirvana. Incorporating Buddhist principles into the interpretation of the Twelve Steps can provide a unique and personal path for those in recovery.

This fusion of traditions not only supports the individual journey of healing but also emphasizes the collective effort of community and shared experiences, reinforcing the idea that recovery is a team sport.

CHAPTER ELEVEN

THE ALUMNI ASSOCIATION: STAYING INSPIRED

THE AGNOSTIC STEPS SERVE AS AN INCLUSIVE ADAPTATION of the original Twelve Steps of Alcoholics Anonymous (AA), designed for individuals who may not subscribe to a specific religious belief or who embrace a secular worldview. They provide a welcoming framework for those seeking recovery without the constraints of traditional religious interpretations.

Acknowledging Our Powerlessness

Admitting we were powerless over alcohol means acknowledging that addiction has made our lives unmanageable and that we cannot control it on our own.

It is time to take an honest assessment of your relationship with alcohol. Think about how it affects your life, your relationships, and your well-being. Write down your thoughts and feelings about your drinking habits. This can help clarify your understanding of your situation.

Talk to someone that you trust about your struggles. It could be a friend, a family member, or a professional.

Try attending meetings. Participate in AA meetings or other similar meetings. Be open and honest. Approach this process with an open mind and be truthful with yourself and others. Vulnerability is the key to growth.

Educate yourself by learning about the AA program and other similar programs.

Set goals. Think about what you want to achieve by addressing your alcohol use. Understand that this process may take time to fully accept your situation.

Be kind to yourself as you navigate this step. Remember that acknowledging the need to change is a courageous first step towards recovery.

Came to Believe in the Need for Greater Strengths

Came to believe and accept that we need strengths beyond our awareness and resources to restore us to sanity; this means recognizing that we need help from sources beyond ourselves to recover from addiction and restore balance to our lives. You succeed at this step by coming to believe that a power greater than yourself can aid in your journey toward recovery.

Consider the following strategies:

- *Explore Your Beliefs:* Reflect on your current beliefs about a higher power. This could be spiritual, religious, or simply a sense of connection to something greater than yourself. Allow yourself to contemplate what this concept means to you.

- *Approach with an Open Heart and Mind:* Be willing to consider new ideas and perspectives about spirituality and support.

Embracing flexibility in your beliefs can open doors to new possibilities.

- *Listen to Others:* Attend group meetings and hear the experiences of others. Their stories about finding their higher power can inspire your own journey. If you have a sponsor, engage in open conversations with them about your thoughts and feelings regarding this step; their guidance can be invaluable.

- *Explore Resonant Literature:* Read literature or spiritual texts that resonate with you. These resources can deepen your understanding and offer insights that align with your personal beliefs.

- *Practice Meditation or Reflection:* Spend time in meditation or quiet reflection. This practice can help you connect with your inner self and explore your beliefs, fostering a greater sense of awareness.

- *Engage with Supportive Communities:* Connect with your AA group or other supportive communities. Sharing your journey can foster a sense of belonging and understanding, reminding you that you are not alone in this process.

- *Accept Evolution in Understanding:* Understand that your perception of a higher power may evolve over time. Allow yourself the freedom to grow and change in your beliefs as you navigate your recovery.

- *Acknowledge Positive Changes:* Concentrate on the positive changes in your life since beginning your recovery journey. Recognize how these transformations can reinforce the idea of a greater power at work in your life. You don't need to have everything figured out immediately; take your time.

- *Take Manageable Steps:* Embrace the second step as a profound part of your journey toward finding hope and purpose. Focus on small, manageable steps in your exploration of this belief, allowing it to unfold naturally.

Made a decision to entrust our will and our lives to the care of the collective wisdom and resources of those who have searched before us; this means deciding to seek support and guidance from others who have experience in recovery and can assist us on our journey. To succeed at this step of Alcoholics Anonymous, which involves making a decision to turn your will and your life over to the care of a higher power, please consider the following strategies:

- **Reflect on Surrendering Control:** This step is about trust and letting go of the need to manage everything. Take time to ponder what surrendering control means for you personally.

- **Clarify Your Concept of a Higher Power:** Understanding what a power greater than yourself signifies is crucial. It could be a traditional deity, the universe, nature, or the collective support of your community. Define it in a way that resonates with you.

- **Identify Areas of Control:** Begin by pinpointing aspects of your life where you may be holding on too tightly. Gradually practice letting go of these elements, even if it's just in small, manageable ways.

- **Start Each Day with Intention:** Dedicate a few moments each morning to quiet reflection or prayer, asking for guidance and strength. Consider writing a letter to your higher power, expressing your willingness to surrender your will and seeking assistance in your recovery.

- **Help Others to Reinforce Commitment:** Engaging in acts of service can solidify your commitment to this step. Volunteering in your community or supporting fellow members of AA can be fulfilling and impactful.

- **Share Your Journey with Your Sponsor:** Discuss your thoughts and feelings about this step with your sponsor. They can offer insights and encouragement drawn from their own experiences, providing a valuable perspective.

- **Explore AA Literature:** Delve into the Big Book and other AA materials that discuss the third step. Understanding how others have interpreted this step can bring clarity and inspiration to your own journey.

- **Participate in Relevant Meetings:** Attend meetings where the third step is a focal point. Hearing the experiences of others can help you feel connected and supported in your process.

- **Embrace the Process of Surrender:** Understand that fully embracing the concept of surrendering may take time, and that's perfectly okay. Approach this step with openness and willingness; doing so can deepen your recovery journey and enhance your understanding of trust and support.

Make a Searching and Fearless Moral Inventory

Make a searching and fearless moral inventory of ourselves; this means taking an honest look at our behaviors and the impact of addiction on our lives without fear or reservation.

To succeed at this step of Alcoholics Anonymous, which involves conducting a thorough self-assessment, consider the following strategies:

- *Dedicate Time for Reflection:* Set aside specific time to reflect and write, ensuring that you can focus without distractions. This is an opportunity for deep introspection.

- *Use a Guide or Template:* Following a structured approach can help organize your thoughts. Common categories to consider include resentments, fears, and personal shortcomings.

- *Embrace Complete Honesty:* Approach this inventory with openness. Acknowledge your feelings and behaviors without judgment, recognizing the complexity of your experiences.

- *List Resentments:* Identify people, institutions, or situations that you resent. Reflect on how these resentments affect your life and your recovery journey.

- *Explore Your Fears:* Write down your fears and anxieties. Understanding these feelings can help you recognize patterns in your behavior and shed light on areas that need attention.

- *Celebrate Your Strengths:* Don't forget to include your positive traits and accomplishments. This balance provides a fuller picture of yourself and can help counter feelings of shame or inadequacy.

- *Seek Support:* Talk to your sponsor or a trusted fellow AA member for insight and encouragement. Sharing your thoughts can create a sense of camaraderie and understanding.

- *Allow Yourself to Feel:* Emotions may arise during this process; embrace them. This is a crucial part of healing and understanding yourself.

- *Review Your Insights:* After completing your inventory, take time to reflect on what you've written. Consider how these insights can guide your future actions and decisions.

- *Understand the Bigger Picture:* Remember that this step is just one part of your recovery journey. It doesn't define you; rather, it helps you move forward with a clearer understanding of yourself.

Admitted to Ourselves and Another Human Being the Exact Nature of Our Wrongs

Admitting to ourselves and to another human being the exact nature of our wrongs means acknowledging the mistakes we have made and the harm caused due to our addiction. To navigate this step effectively, begin by electing someone you trust, such as a sponsor or a close friend in recovery, who can provide the necessary support and understanding. It's important to create a safe space for your conversation, so take the time to clarify your intentions about what you want to share. Choose a quiet, private environment where you can speak openly without interruptions, as a comfortable setting can help ease any anxiety you may feel.

As you share your feelings and experiences, honesty is crucial. Discuss the specific behaviors, actions, and patterns identified in your moral inventory from step four. Be transparent about how these actions affected both you and those around you. Don't just list your wrongs; express how they made you feel at the time and how they continue to affect you now. This emotional connection is key to understanding the impact of your actions.

Additionally, be sure to listen actively to the responses from the person you're sharing with; they may offer insights or perspectives that can help you in your recovery journey. Remember that everyone makes mistakes, so be kind to yourself during this process and recognize it as a significant step towards healing. It's normal to feel vulnerable or emotional while sharing, so allow yourself to experience these feelings without judgment. Following your discussion, consider talking about how you can move forward and make amends, which can help you develop a plan for personal growth. By approaching this step with courage and openness, you can foster deeper connections and take meaningful strides in your recovery journey.

Were Ready to Accept Help in Letting Go of All Our Defects of Character

Being ready to accept help in letting go of all our defects of character means being willing to seek assistance in addressing and overcoming the flaws and negative traits that contribute to our addiction. To navigate the sixth step effectively, which involves being entirely ready to have a higher power remove these defects, start by taking the time to reflect on the character defects you identified in step four. Understand how these traits have impacted your life and relationships, and acknowledge your desire for change. Recognizing your willingness to let go of these defects is crucial; remember that this step is about readiness, not perfection.

Engaging in prayer or meditation can provide the guidance and strength necessary to connect with your higher power, reinforcing your readiness for change. Consider creating a list of your character defects and detailing the specific ways they have affected both you and others. This process can help clarify your thoughts and intentions. Delve deeper into what drives these defects by understanding their roots, as this insight can aid you in addressing them more effectively.

Discuss your thoughts and feelings about this step with your spouse or sponsor, as they can offer support and share insights from their own experiences. Take a moment to visualize your life without these defects—positive visualization can serve as a powerful motivator for your readiness to change. Remember that understanding and enacting change takes time, so embrace the journey and practice kindness toward yourself as you work through this step.

Lastly, cultivate humility and accept that you may need help from your higher power and others in your recovery community to overcome these defects. Consider how you can actively work on these flaws moving forward by setting intentions for specific actions that foster positive change. By approaching this step with an open heart and a willingness to change, you lay the foundation for personal growth and healing in your recovery journey.

With Humility and Openness Sought to
Eliminate Our Shortcomings

Approaching the process of self-improvement with humility, openness, and a willingness to change for the better is essential in this seventh step. Success in this step begins with understanding the true value of humility in recovery. Embrace the fact that asking for help is a strength, not a weakness, and recognize that growth is an ongoing journey. Engage in prayer or meditation, specifically asking your higher power to assist in overcoming your shortcomings. This practice can deepen your connection to your higher power and reinforce your intentions to grow.

To maintain focus, identify the specific character defects you want to address, naming them clearly to give your request for change a sense of direction. Accept that you are not perfect and that change takes time, remaining open to the transformative process. Speak about your shortcomings with your sponsor or a trusted member of your recovery group; they can provide support and insights to help you navigate this step.

Journaling about your shortcomings and intentions to change can also be immensely helpful. Writing clarifies your thoughts, reinforces your commitment, and can serve as a powerful tool for self-reflection. Take time to visualize what your life could look like without these shortcomings, letting this positive vision motivate you to keep working on them.

Look for opportunities in your daily life to practice humility and make meaningful changes, remembering that small, consistent efforts can lead to significant progress over time. Understand that overcoming shortcomings is a lifelong journey, one that requires patience and self-compassion. Periodically revisit this step to assess your growth and your readiness to continue addressing new or remaining shortcomings. Through these actions, you create a foundation of humility and openness, supporting a life of continuous growth and recovery.

Made a List of All Persons We Had Harmed and Became Willing to Make Amends to Them All

In this step, we identify the people we have hurt through our actions and become prepared to take steps toward making things right with them. After creating your list, take time to think about each person individually, reflecting on the impact your past behaviors may have had on their lives. Consider family members, friends, colleagues, and others who may have been affected, allowing yourself to truly acknowledge the weight of your actions. This honesty is crucial in understanding the amends needed to move forward.

As you review your list, prioritize the individuals you feel more ready to approach, starting with those with whom you may find it easier to make amends. This gradual approach can build your confidence for addressing more challenging relationships. Take time to consider each person's feelings, reflecting on how your actions may have affected them. Cultivating empathy can help guide you in finding the right approach to making amends with sincerity.

Share your list and reflections with your sponsor or a trusted member of your recovery community for support. They can offer guidance on your approach and help reinforce your willingness to make amends. Remember that this step is about readiness to take action, not necessarily taking immediate action. Think through how you will approach each person, what you want to express, and be open to their reactions, understanding that making amends is a process.

As you navigate this step, be kind to yourself. Willingness to make amends is an essential first part of this journey, and each effort you make is a meaningful step toward healing both yourself and those you may have hurt. Approaching this step with sincerity and empathy allows you to prepare for the next stage, where these intentions can transform into actions that promote healing and growth.

Make Direct Amends to Such People Wherever Possible, Except When to Do So Would Injure Them or Others

Step nine involves taking concrete actions to apologize and make amends to those we have harmed, except when doing so could cause further harm. Before initiating this step, it's essential to take time to reflect on the specific ways your behavior has affected others. This reflection can help you approach amends with sincerity and a genuine desire to heal past wounds.

Consider whether a direct, in-person conversation, a letter, or another form of communication is best suited for each person involved. When you reach out, express your feelings openly and take full responsibility for your actions without making excuses. Acknowledge your wrongdoing, be genuine in your apology, and be prepared for any response they may have. They might carry strong emotions about your past actions, so listen actively and without defensiveness. If someone isn't ready to receive your amends, respect their space and understand that while you can control your actions, you cannot control their reactions.

When making amends, emphasize your commitment to change by sharing how you plan to avoid repeating past mistakes. This assurance can provide a sense of closure and help rebuild trust. If you're uncertain about your approach, consider discussing it with your sponsor or a trusted friend who understands this process. Remember, making amends is not a one-time action but part of an ongoing commitment to healing and growth.

Approach step nine with humility, openness, and a willingness to listen and learn. While the process may take time for both you and those you're reaching out to, your sincere efforts can foster healing, accountability, and a renewed sense of peace for everyone involved.

Continue to Take Personal Inventory and When We Are Wrong, Promptly Admit It

Step ten encourages regular self-reflection, a key practice to maintain personal accountability in your recovery journey. By consistently examining your thoughts and actions, you can quickly recognize any mistakes and take responsibility for them. Set aside a few moments each day to reflect on your actions and emotions. Journaling can be a powerful tool in this process, offering a space to record your observations and insights.

Honesty is essential in maintaining your recovery. Acknowledge any mistakes as soon as they arise, knowing that making errors is a natural part of life. Approach your daily inventory with humility and a desire to grow. The AA principles of accountability and responsibility serve as valuable guides for this step. Aim to apply these principles in your everyday actions, especially when assessing your behavior and interactions with others.

Discussing your reflections with your sponsor or trusted friends in the program can be beneficial, providing external perspectives and support. If your inventory reveals any harm done to others, take action promptly, following the guidance provided in step nine to make amends.

Consistency is key to reinforcing this practice. Make it a regular part of your routine, as this ongoing commitment to self-reflection strengthens your journey. Recognize the positive changes in your behavior and mindset over time; acknowledging these improvements can be motivating and affirming. By integrating step ten into your daily life, you maintain the foundations of recovery, nurturing personal growth and resilience.

Sought Through Meditation to Improve Our Conscious Contact with the World, Seeking Knowledge of Our Purpose and the Power to Fulfill It

Step eleven invites us to engage in meditation and mindfulness, fostering a deeper connection with the world and gaining clarity about our purpose. Set aside a dedicated time each day for meditation or prayer, as consistency can enhance the depth and impact of your practice. Explore different approaches to find what resonates, whether it's silent meditation, guided sessions, or reading reflective or spiritual texts.

Embrace a concept of a higher power that feels meaningful to you, whether it's a traditional idea of God, a sense of universal energy, or a personal understanding of inner wisdom. Use this time to nurture a sense of connection—not only with a higher power but also with yourself and the world around you. Incorporating mindfulness can help you stay fully present, making your meditation sessions more focused and grounded.

If possible, consider joining a meditation group or attending AA meetings with a focus on spirituality. These gatherings offer encouragement, support, and fresh perspectives on spiritual practices. Remember that spiritual growth is gradual; allow yourself the grace to explore and develop your approach.

Keeping a journal of your thoughts and feelings after each meditation session can deepen your understanding and reinforce your commitment to this step. By integrating these practices, you can enrich your spiritual journey, build resilience, and enhance your recovery through a sense of purpose and clarity in step eleven.

Having Had a Spiritual Awakening as a Result of These Steps, We Tried to Carry This Message to Others and Practice These Principles in All Our Affairs

Step twelve represents a lifelong mission, encouraging us to carry the message of recovery to others and to live by its principles in every aspect of our lives. It becomes both a source of fulfillment and a testament to the resilience and growth achieved through recovery.

To succeed in this step, start by actively engaging with your AA group and support network. These connections offer vital encouragement, accountability, and camaraderie. Be open about your journey—sharing your story and experiences with others can inspire those who may still be struggling, demonstrating that recovery is possible.

Consider volunteering in your AA group or broader community. Service work is a powerful way to reinforce your own commitment to sobriety and foster a deeper connection with others. Practice the core principles of AA—honesty, humility, and service—daily, applying them beyond recovery settings to all areas of your life.

Sponsoring someone new to the program can also deepen your own understanding and reinforce your dedication to sobriety. Continue to grow by reading literature related to recovery and attending workshops or meetings to gain new insights and perspectives.

Regularly reflect on your progress, assessing the impact you have on others. Celebrate your successes and learn from any challenges. Remember that patience is essential—not everyone will respond immediately, but your efforts can have a lasting impact over time. Embracing these actions enables you to live by the principles of recovery and gives back the support you've received, making step twelve a meaningful and integral part of your ongoing journey.

The agnostic twelve steps offer a flexible framework for individuals pursuing recovery from addiction, honoring a variety of beliefs and perspectives. They provide an alternative or complementary path to the traditional twelve steps of Alcoholics Anonymous, acknowledging the importance of inclusivity within recovery.

Rooted in the early influences of AA, these steps also echo the principles of the Oxford Group—a Christian organization from the early 20th century—which emphasized four key truths: honesty, purity, unselfishness, and love. The Oxford Group's teachings shaped the foundational ethos of AA, encouraging individuals to live authentically, serve others selflessly, and cultivate compassion. The agnostic twelve steps extend these timeless values, focusing on universal ideals that support personal growth and healing while allowing for individual interpretations and beliefs.

The Oxford Group's foundational truths emphasize a structured, spiritual path toward self-improvement and reconciliation. These four tenets guided individuals not only in spiritual life but also in personal recovery journeys and inspired the framework for Alcoholics Anonymous. They are:

1. **Absolute Surrender**: This principle emphasizes the idea of fully surrendering oneself to God's will, recognizing the need to let go of personal control in favor of a higher guidance. This surrender reflects humility and the readiness to accept guidance beyond one's own understanding.

2. **Daily Acceptance of God's Will**: Encouraging individuals to seek and accept God's guidance each day, this truth underscores the importance of mindfulness and continuous engagement with one's spiritual beliefs. It fosters an ongoing relationship with a higher power, nurturing trust and commitment.

3. **Confession of Sin**: This truth centers on acknowledging and confessing one's wrongs, both to God and to others. It promotes personal accountability and honesty, encouraging individuals to openly address their missteps and recognize their need for forgiveness and change.

4. **Making Amends**: The practice of making restitution and amends to those harmed by one's actions. This final truth highlights the importance of seeking reconciliation and healing within relationships, underscoring the impact of one's actions on others and the value of taking responsibility.

These truths not only shaped early recovery approaches but also laid a foundation for personal growth and ethical living. The agnostic twelve steps, while offering a more secular path, reflect these timeless values, helping individuals cultivate self-awareness, integrity, and meaningful change in their lives.

The Oxford Group's *Four Absolutes* serve as foundational principles for cultivating spiritual growth and personal transformation. These guiding values encourage individuals to strive for a moral and fulfilling life and are central to the group's philosophy. Here's a look at each absolute and its significance:

1. **Honesty**: Being truthful in all aspects of life. This principle urges individuals to practice transparency, authenticity, and integrity. Honesty is considered a cornerstone of personal transformation, fostering trust in relationships and allowing for genuine self-reflection.

2. **Purity**: Maintaining moral integrity and purity in thoughts and actions. Purity inspires individuals to align their lives with high ethical standards, seeking to act with a clear conscience. It involves setting boundaries that protect one's values and remaining true to what one deems right.

3. **Unselfishness**: Acting selflessly and considering the needs of others. This value emphasizes placing others' needs before one's own, promoting generosity and empathy. It encourages people to seek ways to serve and uplift others, fostering a spirit of community and support.

4. **Love**: Showing love and compassion towards others while reflecting God's love. Love is viewed as the highest principle, guiding individuals to embrace kindness, patience, and forgiveness. This absolute fosters meaningful connections and nurtures a sense of unity and purpose.

Together, these *Four Absolutes* provide a framework for ethical living and spiritual growth, encouraging individuals to strive for a life that is not only self-aware but also grounded in service, compassion, and integrity. These values continue to inspire personal development and are echoed in many recovery paths, where they serve as a foundation for lasting transformation.

The Bible provides a nuanced perspective on alcohol and its use, offering both cautionary tales and teachings that underscore the importance of moderation, self-control, and community. The Old Testament introduces themes around alcohol, highlighting both its potential to enhance celebration and its risks when consumed without restraint, while the New Testament focuses on moderation and the value of self-control within a community context.

In the Old Testament, we find examples like Noah, whose story presents a dual symbolism: his vineyard represents a renewal of life post-flood—a gift and promise from God to humanity. Yet, Noah's lack of self-control after consuming the wine disrupts his family dynamics, emphasizing a universal lesson that even virtuous individuals can fall to temptation. The dual nature of wine here reflects its capacity to bring both joy and discord, warning against excess.

The Prodigal Son story, found in the New Testament, adds another dimension to the narrative of alcohol use. In his journey, the son's indulgence in wine and reckless living illustrates the spiritual and social degradation that often accompanies excess. However, his story also represents the power of redemption, demonstrating that no matter the extent of one's failings, return and renewal are possible.

Proverbs provides some of the most explicit biblical guidance on alcohol, particularly in verses like Proverbs 20:1, *'Wine is a mocker; strong drink is raging,'* and Proverbs 23:29-35, which outline the sorrow, strife, and pitfalls of overindulgence. These verses advocate for moderation and self-discipline, warning against the allure of excess that can cloud judgment, disrupt relationships, and lead to despair. The wisdom literature in Proverbs encourages discernment, presenting moderation as a means to honor God and build healthy, constructive relationships with others.

In the New Testament, the approach to alcohol continues with a focus on moderation and self-control. While wine is acknowledged in communal and sacred settings, like the Last Supper, the teachings of the New Testament, particularly through the letters of Paul, stress self-mastery and responsible conduct as foundational to Christian community life. For instance, Ephesians 5:18 advises, *'Do not get drunk on wine, which leads to debauchery. Instead, be filled with the Spirit,'* guiding followers to seek fulfillment in spirituality rather than in temporary indulgence.

Collectively, the Bible offers insights into alcohol's effects on both individual lives and relationships, presenting a balanced message: while alcohol can have a rightful place in celebration and ritual, it requires discernment, moderation, and a focus on self-control to avoid the spiritual and relational harm that excessive consumption can cause. Through these lessons, the Bible promotes a lifestyle of balance and intention, emphasizing that personal responsibility and self-awareness honor both oneself and the broader community.

These passages emphasize a mindful approach to alcohol, underscoring the value of spiritual fulfillment and the responsibility we hold towards others in our community.

In Ephesians 5:18, Paul's message, *'Do not get drunk on wine, which leads to debauchery. Instead, be filled with the Spirit,'* cautions against the perils of drunkenness, where one may lose self-control and stray from a virtuous path. Paul invites believers to seek a higher form of satisfaction through spiritual connection, fostering clarity and purpose rather than the fleeting escape often associated with alcohol.

Similarly, the call in Romans 14:21—*It is better not to eat meat or drink wine or do anything else that will cause your brother or sister to fall*—stresses the impact of one's choices on others. This verse encourages believers to consider how their behaviors, including the consumption of alcohol, might influence the spiritual well-being of those around them. It speaks to the values of empathy and responsibility, promoting a community-centric approach to living in alignment with one's faith.

Together, these verses highlight a balanced perspective on personal actions, advocating for both personal discipline and a respect for the spiritual journeys of others. This wisdom invites us to foster environments where mutual support and mindful choices uplift the faith and well-being of the entire community.

In 1 Corinthians 6:10, Paul's reference to "drunkards" among those who will not inherit the kingdom of God underscores the importance he places on discipline and responsibility in one's spiritual life. The warning speaks to the broader consequences of a life dominated by indulgence, where excessive drinking may lead one away from spiritual goals and self-mastery.

1 Peter 5:8 reinforces this by urging believers to "Be alert and of sober mind," warning that a lack of vigilance opens one up to potential harm. This passage likens an unfocused mind to vulnerability, a state where harmful influences, symbolized by "the devil prowling like a roaring lion," can more easily take hold. Here, sobriety is seen as essential for protecting one's faith and maintaining spiritual clarity.

At the same time, the New Testament doesn't present a singularly negative view of alcohol. The wedding at Cana in John 2:1-11 illustrates a more nuanced stance, where wine is part of a joyful occasion, symbolizing celebration and community. Jesus turning water into wine shows that when consumed with moderation and respect for context, wine can enhance life's moments without moral conflict.

Overall, these teachings suggest a balanced approach. The New Testament encourages believers to prioritize clarity, self-control, and the impact of their choices on others while allowing room for joy and celebration within healthy boundaries. This view advocates for mindfulness in one's relationship with alcohol, seeing it as a tool that can be a part of a joyous life when approached responsibly but also as something that, if misused, can obstruct one's spiritual journey and affect the well-being of others.

Here's how the four absolutes can be applied in daily life to encourage personal growth and foster positive relationships:

1. **Honesty:** Open, truthful communication is foundational for building trust. In relationships, expressing feelings, concerns, and expectations clearly can strengthen both intimacy and understanding. In professional settings, being transparent about successes and acknowledging mistakes without fear can foster a culture of integrity and mutual accountability among colleagues.

2. **Purity:** Living with moral integrity involves actions that uplift rather than harm. For example, consuming media or engaging in activities that inspire rather than degrade helps cultivate a mindset rooted in respect and positivity. Purity in thought

and action encourages a lifestyle that aligns with one's highest values, benefiting oneself and the surrounding community.

3. **Unselfishness:** Daily reflections on how you practice honesty, purity, unselfishness, and love can build awareness and growth. Practicing unselfishness might involve actively listening to a friend in need, helping a colleague without expecting anything in return, or performing acts of kindness that support others.

4. **Setting Goals:** Create specific, actionable goals aligned with these principles. For example, aim to perform one act of kindness weekly or commit to honest, open conversations with loved ones. These small, intentional actions reinforce the four absolutes and encourage steady progress in personal and professional development.

By intentionally incorporating these principles into everyday actions, you can cultivate a life that reflects honesty, purity, unselfishness, and love, both nurturing yourself and positively impacting those around you.

Keeping a Journal for Growth

Take a few moments each day to reflect on times you practiced honesty or encountered challenges in being truthful. Write about what you learned from each experience. This isn't about perfection—it's about progress. Being open with yourself in these reflections can help you understand your journey more deeply. And if work feels overwhelming, try expressing your need for help rather than defaulting to "I'm fine." Reaching out is a powerful step, and you can steer the conversation towards something constructive, turning a moment of vulnerability into one of growth.

Visualizing Progress Through Mind Maps

Create a mind map for each core value, brainstorming specific actions or thoughts around honesty, purity, unselfishness, and love. These visual representations can reveal areas where you might want to grow or improve, giving you a clearer sense of direction. Think of this as mapping out your own "plays" for life, where each idea is a step towards becoming your best self.

Role-Playing Real-Life Scenarios

Practice with a friend or family member by role-playing situations where you might apply these values. Role-playing can prepare you for challenging conversations or decisions, helping you feel more confident when real-life situations arise. This way, when the moment comes, you'll feel ready and supported.

Daily Reflections and Reminders

Consider starting or ending each day with a short reflection on how you can embody each value in your daily life. Set reminders on your phone or use prompts to help you remember these principles throughout the day. It's about being mindful and intentional with your actions, creating a habit of checking in with yourself and staying aligned with your goals.

Books and Community for Personal Growth

Exploring books on personal development or spiritual growth can offer insights into honesty, purity, unselfishness, and love. Many find inspiration in shared journeys and learning from the experiences of others. Joining forums or groups focused on personal growth and spirituality allows you to share these experiences and gain support from a community walking a similar path.

The Legacy of the Oxford Group and AA Principles

The Oxford Group's influence remains strong today, shaping programs like AA, which emphasizes spiritual growth, transformation, and fellowship. The concept of surrendering and sharing personal experiences with a supportive community has become a cornerstone of recovery and personal growth. By connecting with others, you create a foundation of support, courage, and inspiration for yourself and those around you.

A Secular Perspective on the Twelve Traditions of Alcoholics Anonymous

While Alcoholics Anonymous (AA) has developed its own distinct framework, the foundational philosophy of the Oxford Group remains a core influence. The following is an agnostic, community-centered version of the Twelve Traditions, designed to reflect values of unity, support, and personal growth without religious language.

1. **Unity**: Our common welfare should come first. Personal recovery depends on our shared unity and mutual support.

2. **Self-Determination**: For group purposes, we recognize a single authority—the collective wisdom of our loving community.

3. **Support**: The only requirement for membership is a genuine desire to stop drinking, welcoming all who seek change.

4. **Autonomy**: Each group should remain autonomous, except in matters that impact other groups or AA as a whole.

5. **Service**: Each group has one primary purpose—to offer support and help to those who still suffer.

6. **Non-endorsement**: An AA group should never endorse, finance, or lend the AA name to any affiliated facility or external organization.

7. **Self-Support**: Every group should be fully self-supporting, respectfully declining outside contributions.

8. **Community Service**: Alcoholics Anonymous should stay non-professional, though our service bodies may employ special workers to support our mission.

9. **Simplicity**: AA as an organization avoids hierarchy but may establish service boards or committees directly responsible to those they serve.

10. **Neutrality**: AA holds no opinion on outside issues, and thus, the AA name should remain outside public controversy.

11. **Goodwill**: Our relationships with the wider world are guided by goodwill and mutual understanding, building bridges with all.

12. **Anonymity**: Anonymity remains the spiritual foundation of all our traditions, reminding us to prioritize principles over personalities.

Alcoholics Anonymous (AA) grew organically from the principles of the Oxford Group, particularly those centered around spirituality, personal growth, and community support. Although AA did not receive formal permission from the Oxford Group to incorporate its teachings, the foundational influence is unmistakable. Bill Wilson, one of AA's co-founders, was profoundly inspired by the Oxford

Group's practices, especially the focus on personal transformation and fellowship. Over time, however, Wilson and AA developed a unique framework tailored specifically to the needs of those recovering from alcohol addiction, setting a distinct path from the Oxford Group while retaining some of its core ideals.

Agnostic Principles of "How It Works"

1. **Acknowledgment of Struggle**: Recognize that you have a challenge with alcohol or substance use and acknowledge how it has impacted your life.

2. **Understand the Impact**: Reflect on the ways your use has affected your relationships, work, and personal well-being.

3. **Commit to Change**: Develop a genuine desire to change your relationship with alcohol or substances.

4. **Seek Support and Connection**: Engage with a community of individuals who are also pursuing change. Sharing experiences fosters understanding, connection, and mutual support.

5. **Personal Inventory**: Take time to examine your thoughts, feelings, and behaviors, identifying patterns that contribute to your struggles.

6. **Making Amends**: Reflect on how your actions may have impacted others and, where possible, seek to make amends.

7. **Continued Growth**: Embrace ongoing self-improvement. Set goals, explore new coping strategies, and build healthier habits that support your journey.

8. **Helping Others**: Offer support to others on their paths; sharing your experiences can reinforce your own growth and build a stronger community.

9. **Mindfulness and Reflection**: Practice mindfulness to stay aware of your thoughts and feelings, helping you better manage urges and triggers.

10. **Finding Meaning**: Explore what brings purpose and fulfillment to your life beyond substance use.

Alcoholics Anonymous (AA) faces a unique challenge: balancing its long-standing, traditional approach with the evolving needs of a diverse membership. Historically, AA has provided transformative support for many individuals, though its success rate remains modest at under ten percent. This paradox highlights a tension between AA's adherence to its original framework—honoring the countless members who attribute their sobriety to its principles—and the need to adapt to new understandings of addiction and recovery.

AA's resistance to change stems from its reverence for the program that has offered a lifeline to so many, fostering a deep loyalty among members who have found new purpose and sobriety within its fellowship. Yet, as addiction treatment continues to evolve, with many advocating for more inclusive and individualized approaches, AA finds itself at a crossroads. How does an organization known for its traditions respond to an increasingly diverse population seeking recovery? This dilemma underscores the importance of community dialogue, open-mindedness, and perhaps exploring supplementary approaches, allowing AA to honor its past while remaining relevant to future generations.

CHAPTER TWELVE

THE CHEERLEADER: CONTINUED SUPPORT AFTER LEAVING THE FIELD

Bill Wilson and Dr. Bob Smith, co-founders of Alcoholics Anonymous (AA), brought different yet complementary approaches to the organization that would become a lifeline for countless people struggling with addiction. Their diverse backgrounds and personalities shaped AA's foundation and its principles, blending idealism with pragmatism to create a balanced and effective recovery model.

Born in 1895 to a middle-class family, Bill Wilson pursued a career in business but struggled with alcohol from a young age. His repeated attempts to achieve sobriety eventually led him to the insight that a community and a spiritual approach could be pivotal in overcoming addiction. Charismatic and idealistic, Bill became the visionary behind AA. He emphasized the importance of spiritual awakening as a cornerstone of recovery, inspiring the creation of the Twelve Steps as a pathway to transformation and healing. His focus on the spiritual aspects of recovery aimed to address addiction on a deeper, existential level, fostering a supportive community where members could connect through shared experiences.

Dr. Bob Smith, on the other hand, was born in 1879 and came from a medical background. He was a well-established physician, bringing a more grounded, practical approach to AA. His years of heavy drinking had impacted his personal and professional life, giving him a profound understanding of the challenges of addiction. Dr. Bob's pragmatic outlook and medical knowledge made him the stabilizing force in AA's early years, emphasizing practical solutions and realistic steps toward recovery. Where Bill brought visionary ideals, Dr. Bob focused on the application of these ideas in a tangible, grounded way.

Together, Bill's spiritual focus and Dr. Bob's pragmatic sensibility shaped AA into a balanced program that appealed to individuals from all walks of life. Their partnership combined the transformative potential of a supportive, spiritual community with practical steps for day-to-day recovery, forming the foundation of AA and making it a model for countless recovery programs worldwide.

Dr. Bob Smith and Bill Wilson brought distinct yet complementary strengths to Alcoholics Anonymous, shaping it into the transformative program it is today. Dr. Bob, a physician with a deep commitment to the medical side of alcoholism, emphasized the power of personal connection and helping others as a cornerstone of recovery. He was hands-on, directly supporting those struggling with alcoholism and helping to establish early AA groups. His compassion and dedication to each individual's journey were instrumental in creating a supportive community.

Bill Wilson, often known as Bill W., was born on November 26, 1895, in East Derry, New Hampshire, and co-founded AA with Dr. Bob in 1935. Having faced his own battle with alcohol addiction, Bill was driven by a personal mission to help others find freedom from dependency. In 1939, he published Alcoholics Anonymous: The *Big Book*, which laid out the AA philosophy and introduced the 12 steps, a guiding set of principles blending mutual support with a spiritual path to recovery. Bill's writing became the backbone of AA's approach, offering a framework that millions have since followed. He remained a dedicated presence in AA until his death on January 24, 1971, and his legacy endures through those who have found hope and sobriety within the AA fellowship.

Dr. Robert Holbrook Smith, known affectionately as Dr. Bob, was born on August 8, 1879, in St. Louis, Missouri. His long struggle with alcoholism gave him a firsthand understanding of the challenge, and his meeting with Bill Wilson in Akron, Ohio, in 1935 became the spark that ignited AA. Dr. Bob's focus on sharing personal stories and fostering genuine community support became core principles of the AA approach. He played a foundational role in developing the early structure and ethos of the organization, staying actively involved until his death on November 16, 1950.

Together, Dr. Bob and Bill W. built a balanced foundation for Alcoholics Anonymous, uniting medical insight, compassionate support, and a shared journey to recovery. Their partnership left an enduring legacy that continues to support and inspire countless people around the world.

Al-Anon Family Groups provide crucial support for families and friends of individuals affected by alcoholism. In this context, *detachment* is the practice of emotionally stepping back from the turmoil caused by a loved one's drinking. It doesn't mean turning away from them; rather, it's about recognizing that you can't control or "fix" their behavior. Detachment helps individuals focus on their own well-being and resilience, allowing the person with the addiction to confront their challenges without undue pressure.

Key aspects of detachment include:

1. **Emotional Boundaries** – Learning to separate your own emotions from the actions of your loved one. This means not letting their behavior dictate your feelings.

2. **Self-Care** – Prioritizing your mental and emotional health, understanding that taking care of yourself is vital and empowering.

3. **Acceptance** – Acknowledging that you cannot change someone else's behavior, and it's okay to take a step back.

Through this approach, family members and friends can focus on their own growth and healing, which in turn supports a healthier environment for everyone involved.

In Al-Anon, practicing detachment involves using various tools and techniques that support emotional resilience and personal well-being. Here are some key practices that can help:

1. **Education** – Understanding alcoholism and its effects can offer clarity and insight. Al-Anon literature and meetings provide valuable resources for learning about the complexities of addiction.

2. **Support Groups** – Regular attendance at Al-Anon meetings allows you to connect with others who share similar experiences, offering a sense of solidarity and emotional support.

3. **Journaling** – Writing down your thoughts and feelings can be a powerful way to process emotions and set clear personal boundaries.

4. **Mindfulness and Meditation** – Practicing mindfulness can help you stay present and reduce anxiety. Techniques like deep breathing and meditation promote calmness in challenging moments.

5. **Affirmations** – Using positive affirmations reinforces your commitment to self-care and helps you uphold your boundaries with confidence.

6. **Setting Boundaries** – Clearly defining what behaviors you will and will not accept is essential for maintaining emotional health and protecting your well-being.

7. **Focus on Self-Care** – Engaging in activities that nurture you, such as exercise, hobbies, and time with supportive friends, strengthens your resilience.

8. **Professional Help** – Consulting a therapist or counselor can offer tailored strategies and additional support to navigate your unique situation.

9. **Anonymity** – Reflect on the importance of anonymity within Al-Anon, honoring the program's tradition of privacy to create a safe and supportive environment for all members.

These tools empower individuals to focus on their growth, manage their own well-being, and cultivate a sense of peace amidst the challenges of loving someone with alcoholism.

As you wrap up your exploration of this book, consider fully integrating these principles into all areas of your life.

With the personal awakening gained from these efforts, we aim to share our journey with others, supporting them in their path to recovery. One of the most powerful ways to reinforce your own sobriety is by helping others along theirs.

Reach out to individuals who are new to recovery, offering practical guidance rooted in your own experiences. Emphasize strategies that have truly worked for you, and consider leading discussion groups to foster a space for sharing and support. Engaging with local organizations that focus on addiction recovery or mental health can also provide opportunities to give back and connect.

Offer your time and skills to help those in need. Participate in community events that promote understanding and reduce the stigma surrounding addiction and recovery. In panels or workshops, share your story, focusing on the practical, day-to-day aspects of recovery, and inspire others to find their own strength and resilience.

Use online platforms to share your journey and build a supportive community around recovery. Connect with others through groups that encourage open discussions, where diverse experiences and perspectives are valued. This helps foster an inclusive space where everyone feels safe to express themselves and their beliefs.

Consider joining or starting groups that promote mutual support in recovery. Stay informed by reading books, attending workshops, or taking courses on addiction recovery and mental health. Enhancing your knowledge allows you to offer informed support and stay updated on new techniques that can make a difference.

To maintain your well-being, incorporate practices like mindfulness, meditation, or regular exercise. Recognize the importance of your own recovery and set healthy limits to avoid burnout. Balance is essential: by nurturing your own journey, you'll be better equipped to support others on theirs.

Sotheby's recognition of Alcoholics Anonymous as one of the most influential books of the 20th century is echoed by *Time Magazine's* 1999 decision to name Bill Wilson as one of the "Time 100 Persons of the Century." Since the *Big Book's* first publication, its four editions have sold over 27 million copies in the United States and Canada alone, and it has been made available in braille, large print, sign language, audio formats, and online. With translations in at least 52 languages, the *Big Book*, the fellowship of AA, and the guiding concept of a higher power have collectively offered millions of people a path out of addiction and into a renewed life.

Today, *Alcoholics Anonymous* and the *Big Book* are widely regarded as the gold standard among 12-step programs worldwide. Alcoholics

Anonymous Worldwide Services, Inc. has granted permission for over 400 other fellowships to adapt the *Big Book* and its 12 steps. Beginning as early as 1946, groups like the WANA Society in New York, Addicts Anonymous in Kentucky, and Narcotics Anonymous in California used AA's 12 steps, often distributing them in pamphlet form. By 1984, Gamblers Anonymous was established, and many other groups—including those for overeaters, codependents, individuals with dual recovery needs, marijuana and sex addiction, and even depression—have since adopted AA's steps, counting the *Big Book* as their foundational text.

This book, the charter of the AA fellowship, is a profound treasure, ranking alongside historical documents like the Magna Carta in its influence. In 2007, *Fine Books and Collections* ranked the auction of its working manuscript among the year's top 10 purchases, honoring its profound contribution to freedom from personal oppression. Like the great Charter, the *Big Book* has changed the world for the better, offering countless individuals a path to recovery and transformation. As many AA members would attest, the true worth of this book lies in the lives it has saved and continues to save.

Long-term sobriety presents common challenges that repeatedly surface for anyone on a recovery journey. Recovery is a path toward finding hope and purpose beyond addiction, a complex and deeply layered condition impacting millions worldwide.

While often depicted as a straightforward path, recovery is more accurately a winding road with its share of obstacles, setbacks, and victories. The question of whether someone can fully recover or remains in "perpetual recovery" is both complex and individual.

Recovery is generally defined as a transformative process in which individuals improve their health, regain control of their lives, and strive to reach their full potential. For many, lasting recovery is possible. Elements like early intervention, supportive networks, and access to effective treatment greatly enhance the chances of sustainable change. Therapy, support groups, and lifestyle shifts often empower individuals to reclaim control and build healthier habits.

However, addiction's chronic nature can make relapse a reality even after prolonged sobriety. This potential for relapse highlights the idea that recovery is an ongoing process rather than a final destination. Being "forever in recovery" underscores the need for continuous self-awareness, vigilance, and personal growth. For many, this perspective serves as a reminder to stay mindful of triggers and to remain committed to the work of healing and growth each day.

The concept of being "in recovery" can be a powerful source of empowerment. It honors the struggles individuals face while celebrating their resilience and progress. Many who embrace this identity draw strength from their experiences, using them to uplift others and build meaningful community connections. The support from peers who genuinely understand the journey is invaluable, fostering a sense of belonging and shared purpose.

While complete recovery from addiction is possible, for many, it becomes a lifelong journey. Viewing recovery as both a potential destination and a continuous process reflects the nuanced reality of addiction. Ultimately, whether one fully recovers or remains "in recovery" depends on individual circumstances, the support available, and a commitment to personal growth. Through it all, hope and resilience shine, affirming that recovery is a journey worth every step.

The management of Alcoholics Anonymous (AA) faces ongoing debates about its future, reflecting the tension between preserving traditional practices and embracing modern adaptations. AA, rooted in principles of anonymity, mutual support, and spiritual growth, has long emphasized a structured approach to recovery. However, as societal norms evolve and new treatment methods emerge, internal discussions about how AA can adapt to contemporary recovery needs have become more pronounced.

Traditionalists within AA advocate for a strict adherence to the original 12 steps and the spiritual focus that has been central to AA since its beginning. They believe these core elements are essential for building a strong sense of community and accountability among members. This group worries that diverging from these foundational principles might dilute the program's effectiveness and undermine its core values.

On the other hand, a growing faction within AA supports more inclusive and flexible approaches. They see value in adapting AA's methods to meet the diverse needs of today's members, arguing that inclusivity could help AA remain relevant in a changing world. This group is open to integrating new ideas and practices that align with modern perspectives on recovery, believing these changes could broaden AA's reach and accessibility.

As AA navigates this balance between tradition and innovation, the organization's commitment to its mission remains steadfast: to offer a supportive, transformative space for anyone seeking recovery from addiction.

A growing faction within Alcoholics Anonymous emphasizes the need to recognize diverse backgrounds and experiences, arguing that the traditional model may not resonate with everyone seeking support. This group advocates for incorporating evidence-based practices and broadening the definition of sobriety to include various recovery pathways, reflecting a more holistic understanding of addiction. They also raise concerns about the role of technology and accessibility, especially as the traditional model has faced criticism for its perceived lack of diversity in addressing race, gender, and sexual orientation.

Many members believe AA must actively work to create a more inclusive and welcoming environment for marginalized groups, ensuring the program is accessible and relevant to all. This push for inclusivity has sparked discussions about whether the organization should implement targeted outreach or adjust its messaging to connect with a broader audience.

AA's unique, decentralized governance structure adds complexity to these discussions. Without a central authority, the organization is composed of numerous autonomous groups, each managing its own meetings and activities. While these groups adhere to AA's principles, they have the freedom to interpret and apply them independently. This autonomy encourages a sense of ownership among members but can also lead to variations in how AA principles are enacted from one group to another.

The General Service Conference, which includes delegates from various groups, meets annually to address issues affecting AA as a whole. While this conference helps shape policies and provides guidance, its recommendations are not binding on local groups. This structure fosters a flexible, grassroots approach but also presents challenges in achieving uniformity and addressing modern debates around inclusivity and adaptation within the fellowship.

AA's organizational structure includes districts and areas that help coordinate activities and offer support to local groups. These entities foster communication and resource sharing, yet operate with autonomy.

The decision-making process within Alcoholics Anonymous is shaped by this decentralized structure, which brings unique challenges to addressing modern issues while maintaining unity among members:

1. **Limited Central Authority** – Without a central authority, enforcing rules or making binding decisions is challenging. While autonomy allows groups to operate freely, it can lead to inconsistencies in how principles are interpreted and applied. This decentralized control often results in varied responses to emerging challenges, making cohesive decision-making difficult.

2. **Reliance on Consensus** – AA relies heavily on consensus, especially during General Service Conference meetings. Building consensus among diverse groups can be time-consuming, leading to delays in addressing urgent issues. While this thorough approach ensures all voices are considered, it can frustrate members seeking timely changes, especially when adapting to contemporary challenges.

3. **Geographical Challenges** – The decentralized structure, diverse membership, and commitment to tradition create logistical difficulties in implementing changes across all areas. These geographical and organizational divides can slow AA's adaptability and responsiveness to the evolving landscape of addiction recovery.

Addressing these challenges will require open dialogue, enhanced representation, and innovative ways to build consensus, all while respecting the autonomy of local groups. In the end, this lack of central control might prove to be AA's greatest strength, fostering a flexible and resilient fellowship responsive to the needs of its diverse members.

Being part of a championship team requires commitment, sacrifice, effort, and honesty. The rewards extend beyond personal growth—they benefit everyone who loves and supports you.

Together, we will develop a deep understanding of ourselves, learning to embrace our strengths and weaknesses without judgment. This self-awareness will empower us to make informed choices and guide us toward a more intentional life.

We will gradually free ourselves from compulsive behaviors, finding healthier ways to cope with life's challenges. This newfound freedom will allow us to pursue our goals with clarity and purpose.

Our journey will lead us to foster stronger, more meaningful connections with others. By practicing honesty and empathy, we will build relationships rooted in trust and mutual respect.

We will gain resilience, equipping ourselves to face life's difficulties with calm and determination, ultimately achieving greater emotional stability.

We will find a supportive community that embraces our shared experiences and values. This sense of belonging will provide encouragement and understanding as we continue our paths.

We will discover a renewed sense of purpose, motivating us to contribute positively to our communities and the world around us. By aligning our actions with our values, we will lead more fulfilling lives.

Throughout this journey, we will cultivate gratitude for the progress we make, recognizing and celebrating the small victories. This attitude of gratitude will inspire us to keep moving forward, ever committed to our growth and self-improvement.

We commit to lifelong learning, staying open to new ideas and perspectives. This dedication to growth will enrich our lives, helping us adapt to change with resilience and grace.

We will take responsibility for our actions and their consequences, empowering ourselves to make choices that align with our values. This sense of accountability will foster personal integrity and self-respect.

We will hold onto hope and optimism for our future, envisioning a life that reflects our deepest aspirations. By setting meaningful goals and following a carefully chosen path, we will work toward a fulfilling and enriched existence.

In sharing my story through this book, I hope to offer a glimpse of a possible path to happiness—one that can be reached through a deep understanding of addiction and a commitment to overcoming this formidable opponent. Only through hard work, self-reflection, and perseverance can we find the strength to reclaim our lives.

"Winning and Losing isn't a matter of life and death. It's much more important than that."

-Duffy Daugherty

"The difference between winning and losing is a little extra effort"

-Biggie Munn

"The game that most resembles addiction is The Chinese Finger Trap"

-StillTom

"All are lunatics, but he who can analyze his delusions is called a philosopher"

-Ambrose Bierce

"Keep me away from the wisdom which does not cry, the philosophy which does not laugh and greatness which does not bow before children."

-KhalilGibran

EPILOGUE

SOBRIETY IS MORE THAN JUST ABSTAINING FROM ALCOHOL; IT IS a journey toward self-discovery, healing, and reconnection—with others and, most importantly, with ourselves. Along this path, we learn to embrace vulnerability, accept accountability, and find strength in community. Sobriety teaches us that we are not alone, that our struggles and triumphs are shared, and that together, we are capable of profound transformation.

For me, recovery has been a team effort, guided by love, patience, and resilience. From my wife, Wendy, who stood by me through the darkest moments, to my daughters and friends who cheered me on, and to every person I've met in recovery meetings—you've been my teammates. You've reminded me of the power of connection and the beauty of celebrating every victory, no matter how small.

As I close this book, I want to share one simple truth: recovery is a gift. It's the chance to start over, to write new chapters filled with hope, purpose, and joy. It's not always easy, and the road is rarely straight, but every step forward is a testament to the strength within us and the support of those around us.

To anyone reading this: know that you are not alone in this fight. Whether you are at the beginning of your journey or somewhere along the way, remember that recovery is possible, and it is worth every ounce of effort. Lean on your team, celebrate your progress, and never stop striving for a life that reflects your deepest dreams and potential.

Recovery, like life, is a team sport—and together, we can win.